The New Power of
Women in Politics

The New Power of
Women in
Politics

Kathlyn Gay

—Issues in Focus—

ENSLOW PUBLISHERS, INC.

Bloy St. and Ramsey Ave.	P.O. Box 38
Box 777	Aldershot
Hillside, N.J. 07205	Hants GU12 6BP
U.S.A.	U.K.

*For Karen and Dean Hamilton with gratitude
for their help in research.*

A special thanks to all those in government offices and in political action and research groups who provided valuable statistics and other information and shared their views.

—Kathlyn Gay

Copyright © 1994 by Kathlyn Gay

Library of Congress Cataloging-in-Publication Data

Gay, Kathlyn.
    The new power of women in politics / Kathlyn Gay.
        p. cm. — (Issues in focus)
    Includes bibliographical references and index.
    ISBN 0-89490-584-8
        1. Women in politics—United States—Juvenile literature.
    2. Women public officers—United States—Juvenile literature.
    3. Women politicians—United States—Juvenile literature.
    I. Title. II. Series: Issues in focus (Hillside, N.J.)
    HQ1236.5.U6G37 1994
    320'.082—dc20   94-7527
                                                        CIP
                                                        AC

Printed in the United States of America

10 9 8 7 6 5 4 3 2 1

Illustration Credits: Courtesy of the Center for the American Woman and Politics (CAWP), pp. 98-99; U.S. House of Representatives, pp. 43, 46, 61, 63, 67, 75, 77, 79, 82; U.S. Senate, pp. 35, 53, 56, 59.

Cover Illustration: John Duricka, AP/Wide World Photos.

Contents

1 Decade of the Woman? 7

2 Fighting for Rights and Equality . . . 17

3 Running for Office 31

4 Some Congressional
"Firsts" for Women 49

5 The National Agenda 65

6 Women in High-Level
Appointed Offices 85

7 Winning State and Local Offices . . 97

8 Unfinished Business 109

Chapter Notes 114

Further Reading 120

Where to Write
For More Information 122

Index 124

1

Decade of the Woman?

ELECT WOMEN FOR A CHANGE!
WOMEN POWER!
THE YEAR OF THE WOMAN!

These were just a few of the slogans used to call attention to the thousands of women who campaigned across the United States during the 1992 campaigns for election to government office at the federal, state, and local levels. While the media focused primarily on the presidential campaign, news coverage and analysis also highlighted "The Year of the Woman." The phrase was used in previous election years—1984, 1988, and 1990, for example—but in 1992 it underscored gains women had made politically and referred specifically to the record number who ran for and won election to the U.S. Congress.

Eleven women campaigned for the U.S. Senate in

1992, and five women, one of whom ran for reelection, won Senate seats. In a 1993 special election in Texas to fill a seat vacated by Senator Lloyd Bentsen, who became Secretary of the U.S. Treasury, another woman was elected to serve as a U.S. Senator. Those elected joined an incumbent (a person already in office), Nancy Kassebaum, bringing the total number of women in the Senate to seven. Out of the 108 women who ran for seats in the U.S. House of Representatives, twenty-four newly elected women joined twenty-three incumbents as voting members of the House. Eleanor Holmes Norton, a delegate from Washington, D.C., who does not have voting rights because she represents a district, not a state, was also elected bringing the total number of women serving in the 103rd Congress to fifty-five. (See chart on next page.)

These women are much more than statistics, however; they have a great deal to say about who they are, why they ran for office, how they won elections, what they hope to accomplish, and why they believe women need to be politically active. Their opinions, ideas, advice, and hopes are part of what this book is about. In addition, the book shows how far women have come since they first won the right to vote and the long way women still have to go to gain parity with men in politics.

The Changing Political Scene

Women in the United States have been able to win elections to political office at the local level on a fairly regular basis in recent years, serving as mayors and on

WOMEN IN THE 103RD CONGRESS

Senate

Barbara Boxer (D-CA)	Kay Hutchinson (R-TX)	Barbara Mikulski (D-MD)
Carol Moseley-Braun (D-IL)	Nancy Kassebaum (R-KS)	Patty Murray (D-WA)
Dianne Feinstein (D-CA)		

House of Representatives

Helen Bentley (R-MD)	Nancy Johnson (R-CT)	Nancy Pelosi (D-CA)
Corrine Brown (D-FL)	Marcy Kaptur (D-OH)	Deborah Pryce (R-OH)
Leslie Byrne (D-VA)	Barbara Kennelly (D-CT)	Ileana Ros-Lehtinen (R-FL)
Maria Cantwell (D-WA)	Blanche Lambert (D-AR)	Marge Roukema (R-NJ)
Eva Clayton (D-NC)	Marilyn Lloyd (D-TN)	Lucille Roybal-Allard (D-CA)
Barbara-Rose Collins (D-MI)	Jill Long (D-IN)	Lynn Schenk (D-CA)
Cardiss Collins (D-IL)	Nita Lowey (D-NY)	Patricia Schroeder (D-CO)
Pat Danner (D-MO)	Cynthia McKinney (D-GA)	Karen Shepherd (D-UT)
Rosa DeLauro (D-CT)	Carolyn Maloney (D-NY)	Louise Slaughter (D-NY)
Jennifer Dunn (R-WA)	M. Margolies-Mezvinsky (D-PA)	Olympia Snowe (R-ME)
Karan English (D-AZ)	Carrie Meek (D-FL)	Karen Thurman (D-FL)
Anna Eshoo (D-CA)	Jan Meyers (R-KS)	Jolene Unsoeld (D-WA)
Tillie Fowler (R-FL)	Patsy Mink (D-HI)	Nydia Velazquez (D-NY)
Elizabeth Furse (D-OR)	Susan Molinari (R-NY)	Barbara Vucanovich (R-NV)
Jane Harman (D-CA)	Connie Morella (R-MD)	Maxine Waters (D-CA)
Eddie Bernice Johnson (D-TX)	Eleanor Holmes Norton (D-DC)	Lynn Woolsey (D-CA)

local councils. In fact, during the early 1990s, voters in Pacifica, California, elected all women to govern the city, as mayor and as city council members.

In state government, women have won numerous seats in legislatures, increasing their numbers as state lawmakers by more than five times since 1969. But the percentage of officeholders at the top is small. In 1992, only three of the fifty governors in office were women, and the three women who ran for governorships lost their elections. Only two states—New Jersey and Virginia—held gubernatorial races in 1993, and women were candidates in both races. Christine Todd Whitman won the gubernatorial race in New Jersey, but Mary Sue Terry was unsuccessful in her bid for Virginia's governorship.

According to women who have been or are candidates for the governor's office, the public historically has feared that women in such executive positions will not be able to govern with strength and to enforce laws. But women continue to challenge this notion and the limits to power by becoming candidates for gubernatorial races. "It's time to break the glass ceiling and show that women are ready for executive positions at the gubernatorial level," said one candidate, Mary Boergers of Maryland.[1]

In spite of gains made in recent United States congressional elections, women still are not well represented at the federal level. Women comprise more than half of the population, but in the 103rd Congress, they made up only 7 percent of the Senate and only 11 percent of the House—55 out of a total of 535 seats.

Only a few women have been major party candidates for United States president and vice-president. In contrast, by 1994, six other countries had elected women as heads of national governments, including Ireland and Poland, countries known for male domination of politics and most aspects of society. Turkey most recently chose Tansu Ciller, an economist, as prime minister.

Seeking A Greater Voice

For decades, women in the United States have sought a greater voice at all levels of government. Since at least the 1970s, they have gained political strength through women's groups that have actively supported women as candidates for public office. As women's groups have continued their political organizing, women have become even more prominent in political races, particularly during the 1990s.

Other factors have prompted the influx of women into the political arena. One was the widespread disgust over the way Congress wasted or misused tax funds, the money that citizens pay for the services governments are supposed to provide. Voters wanted incumbents out of office; they saw women as "outsiders" who would work to eliminate corruption in government. Many voters believed women would bring honesty and fresh ideas to Congress.

In addition, because of population shifts, new voting districts had been formed in various parts of the country, creating new congressional seats. Many women were ready to run as candidates to fill those positions and to make changes that would benefit the people rather than those elected to serve. Most of the women who ran for and won office had long been politically active in women's groups and had worked behind the scenes in organizing, raising funds, and managing others' campaigns.

One of the most important factors contributing to women's political gains, however, was the public outrage over the way U.S. Senators conducted the televised 1991 hearings on the nomination of Clarence Thomas as a U.S. Supreme Court justice. The Senate is required to conduct hearings before voting to confirm or deny a president's nominee for the high court. Some members of the committee called Anita Hill, a law professor, to testify on a rumor that she had been sexually harassed by Clarence Thomas when she worked for him in the Reagan administration in the 1980s.

For hours, the all-white male members of the Judiciary panel who were conducting the hearing questioned Hill about details of her story. People watching and listening to the televised proceedings could hardly mistake the caustic tone of voice and antagonistic manner of some senators, who clearly gave the impression that they thought Hill was lying or at the least was fantasizing. Thomas defended himself with an emotional speech; he accused Hill of deceit and the Congress of a "high-tech lynching" of a black man. The Senate, however, voted to seat Thomas on the Supreme Court, where he will be for life.

Although some polls (but by no means all) showed that a majority of Americans at the time believed Thomas rather than Hill, many women who saw or read about the hearings were irate. As one woman in her sixties said:

I've voted in every election since I was first able to cast a ballot and I've always tried to be independent—not be persuaded by political party or gender. But that hearing, which I watched intently, showed me that many men in power arrogantly dismiss women and the problems they have in their lives. I decided right then that in the next election I would vote for as many women as I possibly could.[2]

Apparently many women and some men across the United States held a similar view, and the Thomas hearings helped focus widespread attention on the fact that women in the workplace have long been victims of sexual harassment. At the same time, other issues women constantly face—from problems finding quality child care to violence against women—were highlighted more than they had ever been before.

Candidates themselves, particularly women who campaigned for congressional seats, said in interviews that one of their motivations for seeking office was the treatment Anita Hill received. They were convinced from the hearings that men "just didn't get it"—didn't understand that women were not being heard or acknowledged. Since many women had been preparing for years to run for office, they were now ready to "seize the moment."

Some Gains

Although the number of women in high-level government jobs have been few compared to the number of men who have served, women have been part of many administrations, beginning with Frances Perkins who was the first woman to serve as a member of a president's cabinet. President Franklin D. Roosevelt named her Secretary of Labor in 1933, and Perkins held that position until 1945, throughout Roosevelt's entire administration.

During more recent history, both Republican and Democrat administrations have appointed women to cabinet posts, as well as to other top executive positions. President Ronald Reagan, for example, appointed the first woman, Sandra Day O'Connor, to the United States Supreme Court in 1981. Many women were appointed to executive positions during the next administration of President George Bush. At the cabinet level, first Elizabeth Dole and then Lynn Martin became head of the Department of Labor.

In 1993, President Bill Clinton appointed the second woman to the Supreme Court: Ruth Bader Ginsburg. Clinton also selected three women to be secretaries (or heads) of federal departments and three to fill cabinet-level positions. The president's cabinet helps establish federal policies and makes decisions that directly or indirectly affect millions of Americans.

Cabinet members include Hazel O'Leary, Secretary of Energy; Janet Reno, head of the Justice Department and Attorney General; and Donna Shalala, Secretary of the Department of Health and Human Services. At the cabinet level, Carol Browner became administrator of the Environmental Protection Agency (EPA), which is an independent agency in the executive branch; Madeline Albright was appointed United States ambassador to the United Nations; and Laura D'Andrea Tyson became chair of the Council of Economic Advisors. Some of the women who hold these executive positions will be discussed in more detail in later chapters.

If trends continue, women may hold many more important posts and elected offices in the 1990s, helping to establish the Decade of the Woman in United States politics. But there are still many hurdles to overcome.

Obstacles, however, have never prevented women from fighting for the right to be heard and to be politically active. For centuries, women worldwide have sought and worked for equality. In the United States, women's gains in the political arena today have come about because of the foundation laid by many courageous women—and some men, too—who struggled for women's rights from the 1700s on, and especially during the late 1800s and early 1900s. Many of these activists were ostracized, attacked, beaten, and jailed in their attempts just to gain the right to vote, the first step toward equality in any society.

2

Fighting for Rights and Equality

Until the early decades of the 1900s, many people were appalled at the very idea of women attempting to gain power—considered a male privilege. Women who attained public office usually took the place of their husbands who had died. Their reelection depended on male votes, since women did not have the right to vote until 1920, the year the nineteenth amendment to the U.S. Constitution became effective. Nevertheless, women have long been involved in and at the forefront of political movements, including the movement to abolish slavery, to bring about education and workplace reforms, and to achieve women's suffrage, or voting rights.

"Determined To Foment A Rebellion"

During the 1770s John Adams, later the second

president of the United States, was away from home often, meeting with other leaders of the revolution to write the new Constitution of the United States. His wife, Abigail, often wrote to him during that time about the status of women. In one now-famous letter, Abigail urged her husband and other delegates to the Continental Congress to overturn colonial laws (based on English Common Law) that allowed men great power over women. When women married, everything they owned became the property of their husbands. A woman did not have the legal right to sign a will or sue in court. Her husband had the right to keep any money she might earn, to physically discipline her, and if she fled brutal treatment, to force her to return. Abigail wanted legislators to:

> remember the ladies and be more generous and favorable to them than your ancestors. Do not put such unlimited power into the hands of the husbands. . . . If particular care and attention is not paid to the ladies, we are determined to foment a rebellion, and will not hold ourselves bound by any laws in which we have no voice or representation.[1]

John Adams's response was typical of the time (and still prevalent among some groups today): "I cannot but laugh," he wrote. "We know better than to repeal our masculine systems . . . which would completely subject us to the despotism of the petticoat."[2] Adams believed, as did many colonists, that women's "delicacy" made:

> them unfit for practice and experience in the great business of life, and the hardy enterprises of war, as well as the arduous cares of the state. Besides, their

attention is so much engaged with the necessary nurture of their children, that nature has made them fittest for domestic cares.[3]

Adams was also critical of men who were "wholly destitute of property," which included most nonwhites. In Adams's view, landless men, like women, were "too little acquainted with public affairs to form a right judgment, and too dependent upon other men to have a will of their own."[4]

The entrenched belief, backed by law, was that only men of property should hold and wield power. This created huge obstacles for many groups who tried to gain voting rights and to run for and win political office. People faced harassment, physical attacks, and even death to challenge beliefs, customs, and laws that denied them full citizenship.

Abolition and Women's Rights Issues

During the 1800s, the injustices of slavery and lack of rights for women were linked together by numerous women who publicly protested the bondage of both groups. Two of those women were Angelina and Sarah Grimke, sisters who had been born on a South Carolina slaveholding plantation. They grew up despising the practice of slavery and were forced to leave home because of their views.

Traveling to the North, the sisters joined the Religious Society of Friends, or Quakers, one of the few religious groups at the time that allowed women to speak out publicly. That practice was strongly opposed by most other Protestant denominations; they commanded women to remain silent and to let men dominate. The Quakers also were one of the first religious groups to oppose slavery.

At many public meetings during 1836 and 1837, the Grimke sisters denounced slavery and called for immediate freedom for slaves. Hecklers frequently greeted the sisters with shouts and drum beats and sometimes pelted them with rotten eggs and stones in attempts to stifle their message. Clergy also criticized the sisters, saying their behavior was unladylike and shameful. They quoted biblical verses to underscore demands that women be modest and dependent upon men. But in speeches and articles, Angelina and Sarah fought back; they refused to accept any biblical arguments for repressing women and denying them equality. In one article, Sarah called on men "to take their feet from off our necks, and permit us to stand upright on the ground God has designed us to occupy."[5]

After Angelina's marriage, the sisters and Angelina's husband, Theodore Weld, a well-known abolitionist, compiled and published *American Slavery As It Is: Testimony of a Thousand Witnesses.* The 1839 publication sold more than 100,000 copies within a year. It graphically described the horrors of slave practices and sparked outrage among some religious groups. The indignation in turn prompted support for the American Anti-Slavery Society, which was founded in 1833 and led by another Quaker, Lucretia Mott, and others.

Mott also helped link the abolitionist movement with the fight for women's rights. She had become friends with reformer Elizabeth Cady Stanton, whom she had met eight years before at a worldwide antislavery convention. Mott, Stanton, and several other Quakers organized a convention (or more accurately, a public meeting) "to discuss the social, civil, and religious rights of women," as a small newspaper notice described it. Although the women feared their meeting would not be well attended, the group that gathered in Seneca Falls, New York, in 1848 included three hundred people, about forty of them men who supported the cause.[6]

The organizers had prepared a Declaration of Sentiments and Resolutions, which spelled out the rights women sought. It became a guideline for suffrage groups that organized later. Stanton, who had never before spoken in public, read the document to the assembly. Paraphrasing the U.S. Declaration of Independence, the document condemned tyranny—not of the British king over colonists, but of men over women. It declared, in part,

> We hold these truths to be self-evident; that all
> men and women are created equal; . . . The history
> of mankind is a history of repeated injuries and
> usurpations on the part of man toward woman. . . .
> To prove this, let facts be submitted . . .

The declaration listed proof of man's "establishment of absolute tyranny" over woman, including the power of men to prevent the right of "elective franchise" (the vote) for women and to compel women to "submit to laws in the formation of which she had no voice." Many other grievances also were listed, such as a woman's lack of property rights, education, and positions in religious and government institutions. One part of the document accused man of endeavoring "in every way he could, to

21

destroy [a woman's] confidence in her own powers, to lessen her self-respect and to make her willing to lead a dependent and abject life."[7]

Although the Seneca Falls convention has been called the beginning of the women's rights movement, it did not bring about woman's suffrage. Voting rights were not gained until decades later. But women continued to work for political equity and civil rights. Stanton, for example, went on from the Seneca Falls convention to become a major feminist thinker, writer, and speaker. She helped build a movement that fought for women's rights in all areas of society, including women's right to vote.

Lucy Stone was another activist and great orator demanding women's rights and abolition of slavery. Although from a poor farm family, she worked throughout her teenage years to obtain an education at Oberlin College in Ohio. Founded in 1833, Oberlin was the first college to offer women the kinds of courses men routinely studied, and was the first college of its kind to welcome students without regard to race or gender. After preparing herself for public speaking at Oberlin, Stone went on to become a leading spokeswoman for women's rights. In 1847, the year she graduated, Stone gave her first public address on the issue, speaking from the pulpit of her brother's church in Massachusetts.[8]

Another important activist was Sojourner Truth, a former slave. She is remembered for the eloquent speeches she gave on women's rights. On one occasion in 1851, she asked to address a women's rights group in order to refute the common argument that women always needed assistance from men. Most versions of that legendary speech were based on recall of her words years later. But a news account written at the scene and published in the *Anti-Slavery Bugle* (June 21, 1851) is more likely (in the opinion of history scholar Margaret Washington) to be the address Sojourner gave. The *Bugle* declared that Sojourner Truth addressed the crowd with these words:

> I am a woman's rights. I have as much muscle as any man, and can do as much work as any man. I have plowed and reaped and husked and chopped and mowed, and can any man do more than that? . . . The poor men seem to be all in confusion, and don't know what to do. Why, children, if you have woman's rights, give it to her and you will feel better. You will have your own rights, and they won't be so much trouble.[9]

Other Activists in The 1800s

Along with women's legal and political rights, social, educational, and workplace reforms were a necessary part of the overall effort to achieve political gains for women. After all, if most women were forced to remain like children, legally dependent, uneducated, and with no control over their own income, they could hardly obtain political influence or win public office. Even independent women—those who worked in factories or were teachers, one of the few professions open to women—seldom gave priority to political causes. They had to struggle daily for survival. The majority worked long hours for low wages, sometimes as little as twenty-five cents per day.

Yet hundreds of women found the stamina and courage in the 1800s to help pave the way for today's political activism in the United States. They included Dorothea Dix in Massachusetts, who led impassioned crusades for humanitarian causes. Dix called attention to the brutal treatment of the mentally ill, who were imprisoned, chained, caged, and beaten into submission. Her crusade convinced the Massachusetts legislature to build hospitals for the mentally ill and to improve the filthy conditions of prisons.

Another well-known activist was Jane Addams, a suffragist leader and cofounder of the American Civil Liberties Union. But she is best known as cofounder of Chicago's Hull House, which she called a "settlement house." Here poor, immigrant families could find refuge and learn about American ways. Because of the success of Hull House, many similar facilities across the United States were established. They became training grounds for the nation's first social workers. Many of these social workers also became politically active, helping to pass laws that limited child labor and improved working conditions for women.

In the field of education, women such as Emma Willard and Elizabeth Blackwell helped set up schools for women. They now could take courses that previously had been reserved only for men and could be trained to work outside the home. Willard established a secondary school for girls in Troy, New York, and Blackwell, the first woman to become a medical doctor in the United States, founded a medical school to train women as doctors and nurses.

Although Sarah Bagley is not widely known today, she was one of the first women to lead a trade union for textile workers. During the 1800s, mill owners hired primarily young women from farms. The "girls," as they were called, were willing to work from twelve to sixteen hours a day in crowded, poorly ventilated, and unsafe factories. The women lived in company boarding houses and were required to pay most of their meager wages for board.

At first, the young mill workers seemed to accept their conditions, but by the 1830s wages were cut and work hours lengthened. The factory workers began to protest and organize. Among the organized workers were those at Lowell, Massachusetts. They formed the Lowell Female Labor Reform Association in 1845 with Bagley as president.

Bagley gave numerous speeches and wrote many articles and letters calling for workers to organize, and for the state to investigate working conditions at the mills. Although a state government committee conducted an investigation, the committee members voted against reduced working hours and other improvements. But the labor association did not give up. Instead, workers helped defeat the reelection of a state legislator who had been chairman of the investigative committee. The legislator retaliated by using smear tactics—misleading statements and lies—to discredit Bagley and the Association, which eventually dissolved.[10]

In later years, women became organizers for large national unions or organized labor unions that were affiliated with national groups. Women workers in textile industries, shoe companies, hat and dress factories, meat packing plants, printing firms, laundries, and many other workplaces joined unions in the 1800s in attempts to improve their wages and working conditions. Women also campaigned to pass laws that would protect the health and safety of all workers.

Listings of women and their efforts to overcome the discriminatory practices that suppressed them could fill many pages. Some activists were willing to subordinate political rights in order to advance other causes. But underlying all women's efforts was the knowledge that any social, economic, or other rights achieved meant little if women could not vote or be elected to political office where they could have a voice in legislation and government.

Passing the Nineteenth Amendment

Susan B. Anthony was one of the most famous persons associated with the women's fight for suffrage. Her efforts began in New York during the 1850s. She not only spoke out against slavery but also organized volunteers and traveled with them from county to county in New York. They got signatures on petitions asking the state legislature for reforms in laws that discriminated against women.

Anthony's trip through New York in the winter of 1855 became a legend in itself. She traveled in bitter cold by train, stagecoach, and on foot, tramping through streets and across fields. She suffered frostbite and exhaustion but still collected signatures on petitions, raised funds for her cause, and held meetings wherever she could find a hall.

The first petitions, with thousands of signatures, called on the legislature to pass laws allowing women control over their own earnings, custody of their children after divorce, and the right to vote. Although the legislature refused to act on the petitions and ridiculed the concept of needed reforms, New York lawmakers were more receptive a few years later. Anthony—with her friend Elizabeth Cady Stanton, who addressed the state legislature in 1860—helped pass legislation in New York that established the right of women to own property, to keep the wages they earned, and to sue in court. They did not win the right to vote, however.

Organized efforts to win women's right to vote came to a near standstill when the Civil War began. The battle for the union and the issue of slavery overshadowed suffrage. Slavery was outlawed with the Thirteenth Amendment to the U.S. Constitution, ratified at the end of the war in 1865. The Fourteenth Amendment, ratified in 1868, made African Americans citizens (African Americans were denied citizenship when the U.S. Constitution was adopted). The Fifteenth Amendment soon became the focus of public attention. It stated that a United States citizen's right to vote "shall not be denied or abridged by the United States nor any state, on account of race, color, or previous servitude."

Women such as Anthony, Stanton, and many others, argued relentlessly for inclusion of the word "sex" in the amendment. But other women insisted that once African-American men won the vote, then enfranchisement for women would soon follow. This conflict resulted in a split between activist women. Stanton and Anthony formed the National Woman Suffrage Association (NWSA) to work exclusively for a national law or amendment that guaranteed women's voting rights. Lucy Stone founded the American Woman Suffrage

Association (AWSA), which concentrated on a variety of women's issues. They also worked to pass state laws for woman suffrage, succeeding first in Wyoming in 1890, and then in Colorado, Utah, and Idaho.

The Fifteenth Amendment was ratified in 1870 without guaranteeing women the right to vote. Over the next five decades, the suffrage issue was sometimes buried amidst other causes, but it did not die. These other causes included struggles to improve the wages of women who were working in the ever-expanding industrial system and to break down barriers to higher education and professional careers. Women of color faced additional hurdles. They were subjected to violent attacks and the men in their families frequently were victims of lynchings carried out by the Ku Klux Klan and other hate groups that organized to intimidate freed slaves.

Over 3,300 African-American men were lynched between 1865 and 1919. But in the face of threats on her own life, Ida B. Wells-Barnett, born of slave parents, wrote numerous articles and gave speeches against these murders. She became part-owner of a Tennessee newspaper, the *Memphis Free Press,* which she used to further her crusade. She also criticized the poor schools that African-American children attended and called for improved educational facilities. Later she helped organize the National Association for the Advancement of Colored People.[11]

In spite of, and also because of, the many social and economic issues that needed to be addressed in the second half of the 1800s, the two women's suffrage organizations (NWSA and AWSA) merged. They became the National

American Woman Suffrage Association (NAWSA) and began to work toward their common cause.

World War I interrupted the organized efforts of women to win the vote, but the war also worked in their behalf. Women flocked in large numbers to industrial jobs and worked in government positions that had previously been held by men. After the war was over, women's contributions were recognized. Legislators now had no logical reason to deny the vote to half of the nation's adults.

Yet, it took a great deal of pressure from women's groups to win the vote. Some picketed the White House for days at a time. Finally President Woodrow Wilson publicly expressed his support for the proposed Nineteenth Amendment to the U.S. Constitution: "The right of citizens of the United States to vote shall not be denied or abridged by the United States or by any State on account of sex." Congress passed the amendment in 1919. Fourteen months later, the amendment was ratified by thirty-six state legislatures (the three-fourths required for passage), and women finally had the right to vote.

3

Running for Office

When women won the right to vote, they did not turn out in large numbers to cast ballots. Many women stayed away from the polls because they knew little about politics and accepted the common myth that government, like business, was a "man's world." However, the year before the nineteenth amendment passed, the League of Women Voters was founded—an offshoot of the National American Woman Suffrage Association—to educate women on their voting rights and to encourage their participation in politics. Originally, the League limited membership to women, but in 1974 it began to include men. League activities became more varied also, concentrating on voter registration drives, studies on numerous national political and social concerns, and distribution of information on political candidates and issues.

Along with the League, other organizations have emphasized the importance of women's political involvement and have supported women as candidates. They include the National Organization for Women (NOW), founded in 1966; the National Women's Political Caucus (NWPC), formed in 1971; and the Women's Campaign Fund, organized in 1974. The Center for the American Woman and Politics (CAWP) at Rutgers, founded in 1971, is a resource center that maintains a great deal of data on women in politics and government.

In spite of organized efforts, gains in political power for women have come slowly. Until the 1992 election, a total of only 134 women had *ever* held congressional seats from the time Congress formed in the 1700s. Only six women, including Margaret Chase Smith (1964) and Shirley Chisholm (1972), were contenders on major political party ballots for the office of president of the United States. And in 1984, Geraldine Ferraro, a Democrat, was the first woman to run as a vice-presidential candidate on a major party ticket.

Harriett Woods, former lieutenant governor of Missouri, the first woman ever elected to a high-level office in that state, pointed out that women have "moved up the hard way, from city council to the state legislature and . . . to statewide office."[1] The number of women in state legislatures increased from 344 in 1971 to 1,368 in 1991, according to CAWP.

Efforts to further increase the number of women candidates and to help them win office have continued. Most national political organizations that support women have concentrated on races for federal offices.

But the NWPC and other groups now are calling attention to more local and state races where women are candidates. Prior to a NWPC convention in Los Angeles in the summer of 1993, Woods announced that the organization would "launch a mammoth recruiting of [women] candidates" at every level of government.[2]

The primary agenda of women's political groups is to train women for campaigns and to help them overcome obstacles to political office, such as sexism—seeing women in specific roles based on their gender. As one spokeswoman for a political group noted, if women candidates are "single, everybody says they're gay. If they're married, they're having an affair."[3] A more common stereotype, however, is that a woman is dependent and powerless, thus unable to hold public office or a responsible job.

"Mom in Tennis Shoes"

"You can't make any difference. You're just a mom in tennis shoes." This was what Patty Murray, a housewife and mother of two, was told during her first attempt in 1980 to make a change in government. She had gone to her state's capital in Olympia, Washington, to protest cuts in funds for a public preschool program, but a lawmaker ridiculed her efforts, in effect writing her off as ineffectual. Such an arrogant male attitude is a barrier that many women in politics say they face.

However, the contempt and ridicule did not stop Patty Murray. It spurred her on to become a successful political activist and then a candidate. After her rebuff at the state capital, she talked to thousands of Washington families, who in turn petitioned the legislature and helped prevent the school funding cutbacks. Murray later served on her local school board. She also attended numerous sessions at the state legislature when school policies were discussed. State lawmakers were, in her view, out of touch with the needs of the people they governed. That prompted her to run for the state Senate, an office she won in 1988.

In 1992, Murray again ran for office—this time as the Democratic candidate for the U.S. Senate. With the support of her husband Robert, a business executive, and her teenage children, she campaigned as a "mom in tennis shoes." She pledged to make government work for the electorate—the people—and emphasized educational and environmental concerns.

Murray challenged Republican Rod Chandler, eight years her senior and a veteran of five terms in the U.S. House of Representatives. Chandler attempted to portray Murray as a naive and ill-informed candidate, charging that the state would lose 100,000 jobs if Murray's views prevailed; she advocated cuts in defense spending and increased environmental protection for her state.[4]

But apparently Washington voters wanted Murray's views to prevail, since they elected her by a large margin—the first woman to serve as a U.S. Senator from her state. She also made history just days after being sworn into office, becoming the first newly elected senator from Washington to be named to the powerful Senate Appropriations Committee, which writes the federal budget. Murray's position on the committee could help secure funds for trade and natural resource development in

"I believe that the message of the last election was loud and clear; as a nation we must begin to care for each other once again."
—U.S. Senator Patty Murray of Washington.

Washington and for clean-up of the notorious Hanford nuclear plant, which has contaminated land and waterways in the state. "Those decisions will all come through Appropriations," she explained.[5]

Double Standards and Other Hurdles

While Senator Murray and others have overcome some aspects of sexism in politics, another reflection of a sexist attitude is the double standard set for those seeking government office. A certain type of behavior is expected (and socially accepted) for women and another type is expected for men. For instance, the public wants candidates to show that they are tough and competent and "toughness" is often perceived as the ability to wage war or, at the very least, to have served in the military. Yet in the 103rd Congress, which is predominantly male, only 41 percent of the House Democrats and 54 percent of the Republicans served in the military; in the Senate 66 percent of the Democrats and 64 percent of Republicans were in the armed forces.[6]

Voters also seem to equate toughness with "macho" behavior: not showing emotion such as grief or tenderness and being or acting aggressive. Unlike a man, however, a woman cannot be too aggressive or she may be seen as threatening to men, wanting to take charge. But if she holds back, she may appear inept, unable to govern.

The double standard has been evident in televised debates. According to a report in *Psychology Today*, a study comparing the debate styles of female vs. male candidates found that women usually played by the rules of the game. As a result, however, they appeared "less powerful" than men who broke the rules. A linguist at Arizona State University who conducted the study reported that women in televised debates tended to stay within preset time limits and did not interrupt as often as men did.

Men also were likely to change the subject in a debate in order to refute an earlier argument or to avoid serious issues, thus giving them an edge. Male candidates appeared stronger and more forceful than their female opponents. But those women in office who had trained themselves to use more aggressive debate techniques were able to "hold their own," the study revealed.[7]

Another example of the double standard is the fact that women who cry in public are seen as weak. But that is not true for men. As two psychologists, Dorothy Cantor and Toni Bernay, pointed out in their book *Women in Power*, "when President [Ronald] Reagan read letters from children on television he almost always had tears in his eyes, and Michael Dukakis [a Democratic presidential candidate] was applauded for his emotional tribute to his family at the Democratic convention."[8]

A double standard also applies in media coverage of women in politics. Reporters for the electronic and print media who cover a female candidate are likely to emphasize her position on so-called women's issues (such as the right to an abortion and women's health) and on her ability to win a race. On the other hand, news stories and features about male candidates focus on their opinions about foreign policy, the military, budget concerns, and other items considered to be in the "male domain."[9]

Bias in the media is also reflected in the emphasis on

women's appearance. Seldom have news stories about male candidates included descriptions of their clothing, but reports on female candidates frequently have emphasized their manner of dress. Even in office, women are subjected to public scrutiny of their wardrobe. Republican Susan Molinari, a New York Congresswoman, learned this after she was elected in 1990. During her first appearance in the House she wore a black silk pants suit, rather than traditional garb such as a conservative skirt-suit or dress. The pants suit, she said, set the phones in her office "ringing off the wall."[10]

The High Costs of Campaigns

Money—lots of it—has long been a crucial factor in whether or not a campaign for a high-level state or national office succeeds, no matter whether the candidate is a woman or a man. "If you don't have the money, you won't be regarded as a serious candidate," according to a former state official who has coordinated fund-raising efforts for women. "Money is the major measure of credibility to insiders, the media, to people who shape viable candidates."[11]

Funds are needed to pay for costly media advertising and such expenses as office rental, professional staff salaries, transportation, telephone banks, and printed materials for get-out-the-vote drives. But, "many female candidates consider fundraising to be the most distasteful and difficult aspect of their political career," according to psychologists Cantor and Bernay. Why? Because as the psychologists noted, "Most women learn from childhood that good girls don't ask for things, especially money, or call attention to themselves."[12]

Women who run for office of course have to call attention to themselves and also find the money needed to campaign. Lynn Yeakel of Pennsylvania well understands that fact. A newcomer to politics, she ran in a Senate race in 1992, almost beating U.S. Senator Arlen Specter, who was widely criticized for his harsh grilling of Anita Hill during the Clarence Thomas confirmation hearings. Yeakel found that "the average cost of winning a seat in the U.S. Senate and House of Representatives [was] $3.8 million and $544,403, respectively. . . . Senate incumbents running for reelection had to raise, on average, $12,000 a week, every week, over the course of their six-year term to retain their seats. Significantly more money was required if the campaigns were in heavily populated states like Pennsylvania," she wrote in a 1993 opinion piece for the *Philadelphia Inquirer*.

Yeakel explained further that "Our campaign's top priority during the late spring and summer months was to raise enough money to wage a competitive television campaign in the fall." Although the campaign "raised $4.6 million from 52,000 individual contributors and a small number of political action committees (PACs)," it was not enough. In fact it was a mere fraction of the total $15 million spent on the 1992 Senate race in Pennsylvania. Because incumbents "receive more than 88 percent of all PAC money," they are better able to pay the spiraling costs of TV and print advertising than challengers. "This helps to explain why 93 percent of all congressional incumbents who sought re-election in 1992 were successful," Yeakel noted.[13]

Yeakel and countless other citizens across the nation are calling for reforms in the way national campaigns are financed. Too many well-qualified people cannot run for office due to the massive amounts of money needed to compete. This has had a major impact on women who would like to enter the political arena. Until recently, both male and female campaign donors were reluctant to contribute large sums to women candidates, fearing that the women would lose elections. In addition, men in general earn more than women, and they tend to contribute primarily to male candidates. But that situation is changing, particularly as women's incomes increase and as more women head businesses or organizations and can steer funds toward female candidates.

Women's Political Action Groups

One woman who has done just that is Ellen Malcolm, founder of EMILY's List, a political action group that takes its name from the phrase "early money is like yeast" (it makes the dough rise). In other words, if women are assured of funds early in their campaigns, they have a good chance of raising more money to help them win their races.

Malcolm, who is independently wealthy, set up the organization in 1985 after helping to support a campaign for Harriett Woods, who ran twice as a candidate for U.S. Senator from Missouri and lost due in part to a lack of funds. To help improve funding for women candidates, Malcolm decided to solicit donations from affluent women, most of whom had never before been politically active.

In 1986, EMILY's List raised $150,000 for the campaign of Barbara Mikulski of Maryland, helping her win election to the U.S. Senate. During the next election cycle in 1988, the organization contributed to the campaigns of nine women running for the U.S. House of Representatives. Two were elected: Jolene Unsoeld from the state of Washington and Nita Lowey from New York.[14]

During the campaigns for the 1992 elections, EMILY's List collected over $6 million and distributed funds to various women candidates. As with other political action groups, there are criteria that candidates must meet in order to be funded. For one thing, EMILY's List contributes only to Democratic women candidates who support a woman's right to make her own decisions on reproductive matters, and the candidates must have a good chance of winning. The latter is determined after an interview in which the candidate responds to a barrage of questions about her experiences in debates and fund-raising, how she would react to a heckler in a crowd, and how she would respond to reporters who asked annoying questions at a news conference.

The intense interview may jangle the nerves, but it is one way to measure women candidates. As Malcolm explained, "Because [women] are usually underdogs against male opponents, they must fight to win credibility and display the conviction that they really have a reason for running."[15]

Because of the success of EMILY's List, similar groups have been organized, such as the national organization RENEW (Republican Network to Elect Women), founded in 1993, and Republican Women's PACs in several states. Other state groups supporting Democrats include GWEN (Get Women Elected Now) in Florida and PAM (Power and Money) in New Jersey. There are a wide range of nonpartisan PACs across the United States that support women running in local, state, and federal races.

Although EMILY's List leads all other groups in the total amount of funds distributed to candidates, other national groups in the United States have done their share. For example, WISH (Women in the Senate and House) List, which formed in 1991, contributes to the campaigns of Republican women who are pro-choice in regard to reproductive rights. The organization helped put Republican Kay Bailey Hutchison in the U.S. Senate following a special election in 1993.

NOW is nonpartisan in its funding, contributing to men or women running for political office if they are strong on feminist issues such as abortion rights, economic equality, and efforts to stop violence against women. Cynthia McKinney, Georgia's first African-American Congresswoman, credits the group with providing early financial support—when she needed it—to get her campaign off the ground, which in turn led to her election in 1992.

Character Assets

Even if a woman has large sums of money available for a campaign, she needs other assets to win an election and to stay in office. Self-confidence, persistence, courage,

"It is certainly evident that the poor, minority and rural areas of the South have actually borne the brunt of the lack of any kind of cohesive waste management policy on the national, state and local levels."
—U.S. Representative Cynthia McKinney of Georgia in comments about environmental racism, the practice of dumping toxic waste and other hazardous materials in communities of color.

leadership, the willingness to take risks and the ability to handle losses or setbacks are some of the qualities displayed by the numerous women who have won high-level political office.

Consider Lynn C. Woolsey of Northern California, elected in 1992 to serve in the U.S. House of Representatives. She was divorced in the 1960s and was left with three young children and no child support. Although she was employed, her job paid low wages and provided no health care or other benefits; she needed public assistance (welfare) to help support her family. Woolsey was able to overcome the tough challenges, find a better-paying job, and get off welfare within three years. She remarried, went on to earn a degree at the University of San Francisco, and eventually became the human resources manager for a large firm. In 1980, she founded her own human resources consulting company. She also served for eight years on the city council in Petaluma, California.

Woolsey's biography and former welfare status were the foundation for her campaign, which emphasized not only her honesty but also that she is a survivor. After her election, she again displayed her candor and the ability to stand up for her convictions by appearing at a press conference in June 1993 with her thirty-year-old son Michael. Michael was in Washington, D.C., to lobby members of Congress on lifting the ban on homosexuals in the military. As Congresswoman Woolsey stated:

> I am deeply committed to . . . securing civil rights
> for all gays and lesbians. Last year, my son Michael
> told me who he is—a gay man. The overwhelming
> feelings I had were of love, respect, and pride. I

knew then that we had the kind of relationship I had worked for—one in which my children can share themselves as they truly are, and they can count on my love and support. . . . the ban [against gays and lesbians in the military] is not an abstract issue, it is an intolerable form of discrimination that disrupts American families and homes and prevents our children from being all that they can be. I am not speaking today for my son Michael alone, I am here for the millions of other parents determined to make sure their children share in the American dream.

As parents, we have taught our children to expect that. We ask only that our government does the same and respects the rights of every gay and lesbian American.[16]

Of course Woolsey was not alone on this civil rights issue. During the 102nd Congress, Congresswoman Patricia Schroeder of Colorado, the most senior woman member of the House, was in the center of a national debate on the way the military treats women and homosexuals. As a member of the House Armed Services Committee and chair of one of its subcommittees, she helped focus congressional attention on sexual harassment cases in the military, whether against gays or women.

One of those cases centered on the now-infamous Tailhook incident. The Tailhook Association, a group of both active and retired naval aviators, met at an annual convention at the Hilton hotel in Las Vegas in 1991. Female officers invited to the event were forced to walk through a hotel hallway, a gauntlet lined with male officers who physically assaulted the women, grabbing their

"We are saying enough of stalking the doctors, enough of stalking the clinic staff."
—U.S. Representative Patricia Schroeder of Colorado in discussion about a bill that would make it a federal crime to block abortion clinics or to threaten doctors and clinic staff.

breasts, buttocks, and even pulling off their clothes. The scandal eventually forced the resignation of the secretary of the navy and the early retirement of two admirals as well as the reassignment of other officers.

Because of Schroeder's condemnation of sexual harassment, she was publicly ridiculed in an obscene skit performed by military officers, who were eventually relieved of their command. Yet that has not hindered her efforts to prevent attacks and discrimination against women or homosexuals in the military.

Along with standing up for their convictions, women in politics are refusing to accept the notion that "boys will be boys"—an excuse for disrespectful attitudes and abusive behavior toward women. In addition, women who have won high office are challenging what has been called the "old boys' club" that has long ruled in Congress and state legislatures. In short, women are working to establish power for themselves in order to bring about equity for women in government, the workplace, and other areas of society.

4

Some Congressional "Firsts" for Women

Along with shaking up the men's club that has been intact for so long, women in the U.S. Congress have chalked up some "firsts." Some have to do with breaking down social barriers, such as adding a bathroom for women senators near the Senate chamber (as is provided for men in the Senate) and allowing women easier access to the congressional gym, an all-male facility until the 1970s. Other firsts are more revolutionary, such as the election of Carol Moseley-Braun, the first African-American woman in the U.S. Senate, and the election of Eva Clayton of North Carolina, Carrie Meek of Florida, and Cynthia McKinney of Georgia to the House of Representatives, where they are the first African-American women to represent their particular southern districts.

Congresswomen also have begun to break down the

stereotype that being a woman is a "handicap" in Congress. Instead they are demonstrating their strengths.

Changing the Facilities

"You can always tell when women have gotten a real foothold in some new line of work. They get their own rest room," wrote columnist Gail Collins.[1] She pointed out that any woman who has been in state or national office for some time can tell a "bathroom story"—of not being able to find a facility because all were labeled men only. In fact, the lack of bathroom facilities for women has been used for many years as an excuse to bar women from male-dominated occupations in fields like construction and from certain military roles such as combat.

In the U.S. Capitol, a private rest room near the Senate chamber marked "Senators Only" bars women. Female senators had to use a public facility. But construction of a new women's rest room was completed in early 1993, and the event made headlines in the *New York Times.* Not only was the women's room a first, it also was a sign that another obstacle barring women from nontraditional jobs was on its way out.

A few congresswomen also have challenged the male exclusiveness of the gym and the swimming pool in the Rayburn House Office Building. Former Congresswoman Bella Abzug obtained access to the swimming pool in the 1970s, and in 1985 then-Representative Barbara Boxer campaigned to integrate the gym.

Congresswoman Karan English of Arizona continued that effort when she took office in 1992. As part of her routine to maintain good health, English often plays basketball and swims. But in the Rayburn building she was not welcome in the gym—unless she told attendants she was coming. No male member had to announce his arrival, however. English refused to be treated as though she did not belong and went to the gym unannounced. Since then, she has used the basketball court on a weekly basis. She also has used the swimming pool regularly, even though access for women is through a basement garage door that only an attendant can unlock. Male members of Congress access the pool by an elevator in the men's locker room. There is no locker room for women.

The lack of accommodations for women members is just one more manifestation of the "boys' club" in Congress. Another is the stereotype of congresswomen as staff, guests, or spouses of congressional members. To cite one example: Not long after taking office, Congresswoman Cynthia McKinney of Georgia tried to use a reserved elevator on Capitol Hill and was politely reminded by Lillie Drayton, the operator, that the elevator was for members only. McKinney thanked Drayton and entered the elevator. Again Drayton said, "This elevator is only for members of Congress." Finally, after a third crisp reminder from Drayton, McKinney pointed out her identification pin. As the elevator carried McKinney to her destination, the operator learned that Congresswoman McKinney represented Drayton's own district in Georgia.

One of the most visible and widely publicized new women senators to be sworn into the 103rd Congress was Carol Moseley-Braun. But on her first day in the Senate she, too, was mistakenly slighted. She was given an identification pin with the term "spouse" on it, which she quickly returned to a clerk with the request "try again." The ID was replaced with one bearing the proper title.

Such stories are often repeated because they dramatize that many people still assume women are subordinates or "just a pretty face," as one congressman put it. But public perceptions have been changing, especially as women in Congress (and in other walks of life, for that matter) have demonstrated their abilities to lead and have spoken out on a great variety of issues.

Moseley-Braun's Election

As a senator, Moseley-Braun joined a colleague who represented another landmark election—Ben Nighthorse Campbell of Colorado, the first Native American in the Senate for more than sixty years. Newly elected Senator Barbara Boxer commented that "it [the Senate] now looks more like America."[2]

Indeed, Moseley-Braun was well aware of her place in history and said it was "awesome" that she would sit "in the old Senate chambers where Frederick Douglass, the great civil rights leader, had held forth before the Civil War," a time "when blacks and women had no vote." Her election was evidence that the political process had opened up, she noted in a television interview.[3]

Diversity in the Senate, however, has prompted more scrutiny than ever before of the women who are new to office. Even before Moseley-Braun arrived in Washington, she was criticized in the media for taking an expensive vacation in South Africa, for renting a

52

"One of the biggest problems facing women and children of this country is the problem of inadequate child support . . . every day in courthouses around this country, our nation's children are being cheated out of thousands of dollars that is rightfully owed to them."
—U.S. Senator Carol Moseley-Braun of Illinois in support of a federal law to enforce child support orders.

$3,300-a-month penthouse apartment in a building along the north shore of Lake Michigan in Chicago, and for the high salary paid to her campaign manager and partner, Kgosie Matthews (who is from South Africa). The senator defended herself by saying that she had taken care of the responsibilities of a senator and that no public funds had been used to pay for her lifestyle. "I am no nonsense about my job . . . I try to be honest and straightforward, but I still like to be myself," she said during a guest appearance on a television talk show.[4]

Moseley-Braun's reported lifestyle hardly differs from that of many veteran members of Congress or other long-time political officeholders. As a political scientist in Chicago observed right after the senator's election: "Every time she behaves as a real politician, people are going to be disappointed. But she is a politician."[5]

Certainly when Senator Moseley-Braun was elected she was no newcomer to politics. She had, in her words, "been working in the vineyards for a long time." During the 1970s, she was elected to the Illinois legislature, serving for ten years. In 1987 she became the Recorder of Deeds for Cook County, which encompasses Chicago. She brought the previously inefficient county office into the present century by modernizing and computerizing record-keeping, which saved tax dollars.

One of her achievements while in the Illinois legislature was passage of a law that barred the state from investing funds in South Africa until its system of apartheid—separating whites from people of color—had been dismantled. She also sponsored and supported legislation to reform education in Illinois and to ban discrimination in housing and private clubs.

After joining the U.S. Senate, Moseley-Braun and another first-term Senator, Dianne Feinstein of California, became the first two female members of the Judiciary Committee, the panel so widely criticized for its conduct during the Clarence Thomas hearings. Moseley-Braun also was appointed to the Banking, Housing and Urban Affairs Committee and the Small Business Committee—appointments she expects will translate into benefits for her constituents.

Women "Deans" of the Senate

Before the 103rd Congress convened, two women held Senate seats: Republican Nancy Kassebaum of Kansas and Democrat Barbara Mikulski of Maryland. Both women made breakthroughs and political history when they were elected.

Nancy Landon Kassebaum was the first woman to be elected to the U.S. Senate on her own merits, without assuming office as the widow of a congressman. Kassebaum's interest in politics was sparked during her early childhood. Her father, Alfred M. Landon, was a well-known politician—a Kansas governor from 1933 to 1937 and the Republican nominee for United States president in 1936.

The Landon family often "held political discussions around the dinner table." As a young girl, Nancy enjoyed "following the issues of the day," when politicians and reporters came to visit her father, she told an interviewer.

"I'd be happy to speak on substantive issues, but to be treated as a bauble on a tree is not particularly constructive."
—U.S. Senator Nancy Kassebaum of Kansas in comments to Republican leaders prior to the 1984 Republican Convention.

But she said, "I never ever thought that I would be . . . a candidate myself."[6]

Kassebaum maintained her interest in politics during her college years and while she was married and raising four children. But she did not actually enter the political arena until after she separated from her husband. In 1975, she left the family farm outside Wichita and went to Washington, D.C., with three of her four children— the eldest was in college—and took a job as legislative aide to Kansas Senator James Pearson. When Pearson decided to retire at the end of his term in 1978, Kassebaum, with the support of most of her family, joined eight other candidates for the vacated Senate seat.

Kassebaum won the election in 1978, and she has been reelected twice, beginning her third six-year term in 1990. She is a popular senator, primarily because she is respected for her independent thinking and because of her ability to build coalitions. Principles take priority over politics in many of Kassebaum's decisions, say both her supporters and critics.

Although for many years she was only one of two women in the U.S. Senate, she has not allowed her party to use her as a symbol of female power or to tout "women's issues." Her aides say that "Senator Kassebaum does not consider issues before the Congress as gender-based. Rather, the issues are concerns that affect a broad spectrum of citizens."[7]

Senator Mikulski also shares that view in many ways. She has long been seen as a champion of the people, particularly working-class people. However, she also has been a strong advocate of women candidates for congressional office.

Mikulski was elected to the U.S. Senate in 1986, becoming the first Democratic woman to hold a Senate seat not previously held by her husband. In 1992, she was reelected for a second term with 71 percent of the vote.

A no-nonsense senator, Mikulski is the great-granddaughter of Polish immigrants; during her teenage years she worked in the family's neighborhood grocery store. Her interest in political activism began during her years at the University of Maryland's School of Social Work and Western Maryland College, where she earned a master's degree. But her political career started in Baltimore when she organized her neighbors to prevent the construction of a sixteen-lane highway through an historic area and a neighborhood of black-owned homes, the first such community in the city. The community activists stopped the highway construction and formed a coalition that helped elect Mikulski to the City Council of Baltimore in 1971.

Five years later, Mikulski won election to the U.S. House of Representatives, serving for ten years. During her first term as U.S. Senator, she was appointed to the powerful Appropriations Committee, which determines how federal tax money will be spent. In her second term, she has continued to work on the Appropriations Committee, and on such issues as prohibiting sex bias and sexual harassment in federal agencies and pressing for environmental cleanup of military bases. She also has maintained her practice of returning to her "home base" on a regular basis. In her words: "The people are my best advisers."[8]

"Workplace discrimination and sexual harassment unfortunately still flourish in the federal workplace . . . each federal department and agency and the U.S. Postal Service should establish a written policy on how it will deal with violations of laws against discrimination and sexual harassment."
—U.S. Senator Barbara Mikulski of Maryland.

House Breakthroughs

Women in the U.S. House of Representatives also have made breakthroughs. When elected in 1992, Lucille Roybal-Allard of California became the first Mexican-American woman in the House, and Nydia Velazquez of New York became the first woman of Puerto Rican descent to serve in Congress. Ileana Ros-Lehtinen from Florida is one more Latina in the House and was elected to a third term in 1992.

Those who set examples prior to the Decade of the Woman include Cardiss Collins of Illinois. When elected for her tenth term in 1992, she gained the distinction of serving longer than any other member of African-American ancestry in Congress. During her earlier years in the House, she chaired the Congressional Black Caucus, a group of African-American members—both men and women—who meet on a regular basis to discuss legislation and policy matters of common interest.

Another veteran of the House is Patsy T. Mink of Hawaii, first elected in 1964 and serving until 1977. She ran for the Senate in 1978, but she lost that bid and spent the next twelve years in various political offices, including the Honolulu City Council. She was elected to the House again in 1990 and reelected in 1992.

With both seasoned and newly elected women joining forces, there have been some signs of reform in the way Congress operates and spends money. One example was the successful drive to disband four House select committees that cost taxpayers $3.69 million a year. First-term Congresswoman Deborah Pryce from Ohio

"The educational difficulties experienced by Native Hawaiians are the result of interrelated health, social and economic problems caused by discrimination, exploitation, and repression imposed upon this community since its domination by the United States in 1893. . . . Future generations of Native Hawaiian children depend upon our ability . . . to address their dire need for education services."
—U.S. Representative Patsy T. Mink of Hawaii before a congressional hearing on Native American education programs.

led the effort, calling the select committees "useless," because "they have no legislating authority. They are used primarily to bolster the members who sit on them and give them added publicity. Other standing [permanent] committees will and should take up the work," she declared. Although the savings in tax funds will hardly make a dent in a federal debt of $300 billion, the "symbolic victory" was important, according to Pryce, because it set an example.[9]

Many other new members of Congress also worked on congressional reforms after taking office. Tillie Fowler of Florida, for example, supported efforts to pass legislation that limits the terms of congressional members. Maria Cantwell of Washington state helped shape a proposal to cut the amount allocated for legislators' office expenses.

But congresswomen have other goals as well, such as providing jobs for people in their districts or protecting their area's natural resources. Many congresswomen have emphasized their desire to make a difference and to be a representative of the people rather than a professional politician who is only interested in the pay and prestige. Congresswoman Elizabeth Furse is one in that category.

Born in Nairobi, Kenya (Africa), to British parents, Furse became a United States citizen in 1972. She never held public office before her election to the House in 1992. But in addition to her work with the Helvetia Vineyards that she and her husband own in Hillsboro, Oregon, Furse has spent most of her adult life in community activism. She has worked for human rights, peace, justice, and environmental responsibility. For six

"This is the people's place." —U.S. Representative Elizabeth Furse of Oregon in reference to the U.S. House.

years in the 1980s, Furse worked with a Native American organization that successfully lobbied the U.S. Congress to pass laws restoring legal status to three Oregon tribes. With legal status, tribal governments are recognized as sovereign nations, and each can relate on a government-to-government basis with the United States government.

After her election to the U.S. House, Congresswoman Furse emphasized that the House is "the people's place." But like many newcomers in Washington, she quickly learned that established procedures and the power of senior members of Congress often stand in the way of changes that might benefit citizens. That, however, did not discourage her and she began her congressional term as an attentive listener and learner. As she explained: "When you're elected to represent everybody, you must listen. You don't have to follow the ideas of every group, [but] even people I disagree with might tell me something I need to know."[10]

5

The National Agenda

After a record number of women were elected to the 103rd Congress, political consultant Ann Lewis predicted that the congresswomen in the chambers would "change the whole culture of the place. . . . You won't see so-called women's legislation shunted aside. For the first time you'll hear speeches about abortion and child care and family leave made by people, women, with a degree of authority."[1]

Even as women in elected office champion what have been labeled "women's causes," they also concentrate on such broad-based concerns as education reform, job creation, urban blight, and international trade. In addition, they tend to the specific interests of their constituents—the people who voted for them. Many of those constituents are, of course, women who have turned out in record numbers to help elect other women to Congress.

Congressional Caucus for Women's Issues

Because Congress has long been indifferent to women's concerns, congresswomen especially want to state their case—not only about abortion, child care, and family leave but also about such issues as women's health, women in military combat, sexual harassment, and violence against women. In recent years, these and other concerns have been part of the agenda of the Congressional Caucus for Women's Issues, which was founded in the late 1970s. It is headed today by co-chairs, one from each party, Democrat Patricia Schroeder and Republican Olympia Snowe. Nearly all of the women in the House, plus some congressmen who support equity for women, are part of the caucus.

Because some congresswomen have long been against laws providing reproductive rights for women (which may or may not include a decision to have an abortion if needed or wanted), the Congressional Caucus for Women's Issues did not take a stand on this issue until the 1992 elections. At that time, members endorsed a proposed Freedom of Choice Act, which would restore the reproductive rights women won in a 1973 U.S. Supreme Court decision known as *Roe* v. *Wade.* In that decision, the High Court struck down state laws that severely restricted abortion, ruling that the laws were unconstitutional and violated a woman's right to privacy. As a result of the ruling, pregnant women could legally have an abortion during the first three months of

"We are not a homogenous group. But the fact that the caucus works well together should be an example of our political maturity."
—U.S. Representative Olympia Snowe of Maine, speaking about the women's political caucus.

a pregnancy, but states could regulate abortion after that period to protect a woman's health.

However, in the 1980s and early 1990s, some states passed laws to more strictly regulate abortions. Those restrictions included limiting the use of tax funds to pay for abortions for poor women on welfare, and requiring young women who are legally minors (usually under age eighteen) to notify or obtain permission from a parent or guardian for an abortion. Most of the restrictions and efforts to ban abortions in some states have been supported by conservative religious groups whose members believe abortion is murder. Other religious groups, however, believe that the choice for an abortion is a woman's to make.

As Congresswoman Schroeder pointed out in a 1992 interview:

> I grew up thinking that this country was big enough for more than one religion, more than one belief, and we now have some real zealots who say it isn't, that there can only be one religion, one belief, one opinion, when it comes to the area of choice. And when you look at the area of choice, it really is so much broader than abortion.[2]

The Freedom of Choice Act

In the opinion of a majority of justices on the U.S. Supreme Court, some of the state laws restricting *Roe* v. *Wade* were constitutional and could stand. Thus only a federal law passed by Congress could set a federal standard in regard to abortion. A Freedom of Choice Act, as proposed, would outlaw the state restrictions. But some members of Congress have drafted amendments to the act that would prevent federal funding for abortions and would include the requirement that minors notify parents or guardians.

Although anti-abortion groups across the United States adamantly oppose the Freedom of Choice Act, many women's groups support the proposed law. This was clear during a political rally sponsored by the National Organization for Women (NOW) in the spring of 1993. Julia Scott of the National Black Women's Health Project (NBWHP) declared: "The Freedom of Choice Act was originally conceived to be for all women. . . . The theoretical right to abortion is meaningless if poor women do not have the financial means to make a choice." Speaking for the NBWHP, Scott said, "We believe reproductive freedom is basic to the lives of all women including the most vulnerable women in our society, poor women."[3]

Echoing those views were representatives of such groups as the YWCA of the U.S.A., the Religious Coalition for Abortion Rights, and the Fund for a Feminist Majority. These groups also have pledged support for the Freedom of Access to Clinic Entrances Act, a proposed law that would protect women and medical personnel from anti-abortion extremists who harass and sometimes physically assault those trying to enter clinics.

Since the 1980s, extremists have bombed clinics, threatening life while proclaiming to be pro-life. They have also harassed abortion providers in their homes. In 1993, extremists shot and injured one doctor and murdered two other doctors who worked in abortion clinics, and in 1994 killed another doctor who performed abortions.

Along with supporting federal legislation, some

members of Congress have worked to overturn federal policies that discriminate against women who want a legal abortion. Senator Barbara Mikulski, for example, led the way for the Senate Appropriations Committee to restore health insurance coverage for abortions for more than three million federal workers. Previous administrations had banned such coverage unless the life of the pregnant woman was endangered.

Support for Family Leave

Congresswomen also have been changing the way arguments are made in Congress. Women generally frame topics in terms of real lives while men discuss issues in terms of statistics and economics. This was evident in the debate on the Family and Medical Leave Act. The law passed in both the House and Senate during the 102nd Congress, but President George Bush vetoed the bill. The Bush administration and many in Congress argued that the law would result in high costs for employers, although there were no provisions in the act to pay workers for a family or medical leave.

The Family and Medical Leave Act became law in 1993 and now provides workers with a minimum job guarantee, prohibiting employers from firing workers who take unpaid leave—time off—for the birth, adoption, or serious illness of a child or to care for a dependent family member. It also protects a worker who has a serious health condition requiring a temporary leave.

Prior to the vote on the act in the Senate, newly

elected Senator Patty Murray argued in human terms for the law:

> As a state senator, I spent a great deal of time and energy on this issue because of a friend who faced a personal family crisis. A mother of a 16-year-old son, dying of leukemia, was forced to make a choice between taking time off to be with her son in his final few months or losing her job. . . . At a time when hospital bills and doctor bills were piling up, she had to choose between her paycheck and her son. That was not right.

Murray also described situations in her own family when a medical leave policy would have helped protect her job. One of those situations was during her first pregnancy when she said, "I was working out of economic necessity, [but] there were no options [then] for working mothers." Women usually lost their jobs when they left because of pregnancy and to care for an infant. They also faced loss of employment if they left to care for critically ill family members.

Murray argued that the Family and Medical Leave Act was sound economic and social policy because it sent a clear message that families were as important as jobs. "Those of us struggling to raise our families and care for the people we love are the backbone of our economy. And when we can care for those we love when they are critically ill—without fear of losing our jobs, our nation will have taken a giant step toward being a caring nation," Murray stated.[4]

After the law passed, Senator Barbara Boxer told participants at the National Women's Political Caucus convention held in the summer of 1993 that "It was the women senators who explained what it was to have to make that horrible choice between family and work. . . . We were able to explain how we had to hide our pregnancies years ago because we didn't want the boss to find out, how we had to leave our jobs. . . . We weren't just talking about statistics, we were talking about our own lives," she told a reporter.[5]

Health Equity Issues

A major national concern for many congresswomen has been the issue of women's health, and they have supported the proposed Women's Health Equity Act of 1991. The Act is actually a package of twenty-two bills that address women's health concerns in the areas of research, health services, and prevention of health problems. As part of that effort and in support of the Act, Congresswoman Patsy T. Mink of Hawaii introduced legislation in 1991 that called for increased funds for the National Cancer Institute to conduct research on ovarian cancer. Mink in her address to the House said that "ovarian cancer is one of the deadliest cancers affecting women . . . and kills most of the women who are diagnosed" because the disease is difficult to detect at the early stages.[6]

By the time ovarian cancer is diagnosed, it is in advanced stages and the outcome is usually fatal. An estimated 21,000 women per year are diagnosed with the disease, and about two-thirds of that number die from ovarian cancer.[7]

Mink has continued to fight for additional funding for ovarian cancer research as well as studies on other cancers that affect women in particular, such as breast and cervical cancer. In addition, she and other women in Congress have advocated health research that is designed to address women's needs. Although those needs are not the same as men's, the health treatment of women frequently has been based on research conducted on male participants in studies. And the research has for the most part been designed, conducted, and interpreted by men.

Evidence of gender bias in health research was clearly shown in studies reviewed in a 1993 issue of *The New England Journal of Medicine*. When it comes to diseases that affect both men and women, "most clinical trials have been heavily, if not exclusively, weighted toward men," the executive editor of the *Journal* reported.[8] Why has this been the case? Because for centuries most research in the biological and social sciences has been designed to show that women differ from men. In other words, the male body has been seen as the norm, so the female body has been measured against that standard and been treated accordingly. In addition, there have been concerns about the effects of drugs on women taking part in clinical tests; for example, no one could be sure whether experimental drugs would disrupt or adversely affect a woman's reproductive cycle.

"It took a report by the General Accounting Office and the repeated strong outcry from the Congressional Caucus for Women's Issues, doctors and researchers," to establish the premise that women's health concerns have to be treated differently than those of men, declared Congresswoman Rosa L. DeLauro of Connecticut in a 1993 speech.[9]

DeLauro, who was first elected to the House in

1991, worked along with Mink and other members of the Women's Caucus "to provide serious resources to the National Cancer Institute for work on breast, ovarian and cervical cancer." For DeLauro this was a personal issue. She is, as she explained, "one of the small minority that has survived ovarian cancer. I was diagnosed, by chance . . . [and] was hospitalized three times and struggled through radiation treatment. The experience gave me life and changed it at the same time . . . it has given me a sense of purpose."[10]

That purpose has been to bring about changes at the federal level to provide health equity for women. Some progress has been made. By 1993, an Office on Women's Health Research had been established at the National Institutes of Health, funding had been increased for women's health research, and four women, including DeLauro, had been appointed to the House committee that oversees funding for health research.

Other Efforts on Behalf of Women

Women in Congress have prodded, lectured, argued, and voted for other legislation and programs that directly benefit women and their families, such as stricter enforcement of laws requiring equal pay for women who perform the same jobs as men. Women have entered the workforce in large numbers in recent decades and have made some gains in top jobs, but they earn one-third less than their male counterparts, according to a 1993 report from the National Association for Female Executives (NAFE). Even in traditionally female occupations (nursing and bookkeeping, for example), women earn less

"We must put an end to the trend in Washington . . . that has shifted the cost of government to states and local communities without regard to the consequences."
—U.S. Representative Rosa DeLauro of Connecticut.

than men. NAFE found, for example, that "male nurses were paid 10 percent more than female nurses; male bookkeepers, 16 percent more than female bookkeepers."[11]

Congresswomen also have pressured for equal opportunities for women in education, and gender equity in sports programs. They have also called for increased federal funding for child-care facilities. They have championed the proposed Equal Rights Amendment, which was first drafted in 1923 and in its present form states "equality of rights under the law shall not be denied or abridged by the United States nor by any State on account of sex." In addition, some congresswomen support the restoration of a federally funded national commission on equity for women. The commission existed from 1961 to 1980 but was abolished during the Reagan administration. If restored, the commission would hold public meetings, investigate accusations of discriminatory practices against women, write proposals for laws that protect the rights of women, and monitor the hiring and other gender-related policies of various governmental agencies and departments.

Women in the House have strongly supported the federal laws to reduce and prevent violence against women and to provide funds for programs that assist victims of violence. Representative Deborah Pryce of Ohio explained why she endorses such legislation:

> As a former judge, I am well aware of the rising tide of violence which is targeted at women and the destructive impact such crime has on families and society . . . three out of four women will be victims of a violent crime during their lifetime.

"I can think of no more important task ahead of the Congress than congressional reform. If we learned anything at all from the last election it is that the American people expect us to have our own House in order, and to lead by example!"

—U.S. Representative Deborah Pryce of Ohio.

One in three women will be a victim of rape during her lifetime. And, between three to four million women are battered by their husbands or partners each year. These statistics tell us that action must be taken to put an end to violence against women. Congress should take the lead.[12]

At Work for Constituents

Besides calling attention to women's concerns over the past few years, congresswomen have been working diligently in both the Senate and the House on problems that affect people of both genders across the United States. High on the list are unemployment, crime, and drug abuse. Affordable health care and environmental damage are other concerns. So are urban blight and deteriorating cities.

Representative Maxine Waters of California is one congresswoman who has spearheaded efforts to tackle urban ills. She pointed out in a floor speech in January 1993 that decaying cities can have a profound impact on the economy and well-being of an entire nation. "America's cities are the spoke of a wheel that includes neighboring suburbs and smaller cities in tightly woven metropolitan economies," she said, adding that "seventy-five percent of Americans live in urban areas, earning 83 percent of our national income. So, too, do half the nation's poor—twice the percentage of thirty years ago. Cities provide high-paying jobs for their surrounding metro areas. They stand as centers of education, culture, medicine, and commerce."[13]

But many urban areas are in economic, social, cultural, and political turmoil. Waters is well aware of the

"If we are serious about tackling our urban ills, we've got to start with joblessness. The best social program is a job."
—U.S. Representative Maxine Waters of California in a speech on "An Urban Agenda for America."

challenges and the needs. The district she represents includes South Central Los Angeles, which was the site of an uprising in 1991. For years, first in the California state legislature and since 1990 in the U.S. House, Congresswoman Waters has fought for urban economic development and similar programs that address inner-city problems.

In 1993, Waters called for "An Urban Agenda for America . . . designed to address the crises tearing at cities across the country." Waters proposed transferring federal funds from the Defense Department to urban programs that provide "comprehensive social service centers"—facilities that offer counseling on pregnancy and substance abuse, decent child care and health services, plus job training. Neighborhood infrastructure projects—repairing roads, bridges, and so on—"would provide jobs for low-skilled workers in their own communities." Another part of the agenda would require banks and other lending institutions to make a specified amount of money available for home mortgages and small business loans in low-income neighborhoods. Finally, Waters proposed tax credits for defense industries that convert to production of civilian goods, which would provide jobs for people in urban areas.[14]

Women who represent Pacific Northwest districts in the U.S. House have taken the lead in a variety of environmental concerns and in the protection of industries such as fisheries, lumbering, and shipbuilding. Six-term Representative Jolene Unsoeld of Washington state, for example, worked for three years to establish a 1991 United States policy banning large-scale driftnets. These thirty- to forty-mile-long fishing nets were used primarily by Japanese, Korean, and other Asian fishermen. The nets capture not only fish that are legally allowed but also illegal fish such as salmon, plus seabirds and marine mammals. Unsoeld helped lobby United Nations members to pass a resolution banning driftnet fishing worldwide. And she was one of the authors of a United States law, passed in 1992, that enforces the U.N. ban and takes away port privileges from fishermen engaged in the illegal use of driftnets.

Unsoeld and other congressional leaders representing districts of the Pacific Northwest also helped pass a federal law that bans the export of logs from state-owned lands. The logs were sold to other countries rather than to small, independent mills in the Northwest. States like Washington and Oregon could benefit financially from log exports, since overseas mills pay about twice what United States mills pay for raw logs. But any increased revenue would be counterproductive because of lost jobs—local mills have to shut down if they do not have raw materials. Thus, selling logs from state-owned land to United States mills helps protect an estimated 5,000 to 6,000 American jobs in the timber industry.[15]

Other congresswomen have authored and endorsed a variety of federal legislation, ranging from agricultural bills to international trade laws. They have served on congressional committees where decisions are made on such matters as the budget deficit, defense, foreign policy, and tax reform. Whatever their efforts, there is little doubt that they will be heard.

As Senator Edward Kennedy of Massachusetts explained: "When I first came here [to the Senate], you waited two years to speak. Now the world is entirely

"We can't afford to return to the days when state lands were used as tree farms for the Far East."
—U.S. Representative Jolene Unsoeld of Washington in a floor speech calling for a ban on export of logs from Washington state to Asian countries.

different." He was referring to the record number of women elected to Congress in 1992 and specifically to Senator Dianne Feinstein's election. California's first woman senator took office two months before other newly elected officials, because she was filling an unexpired term vacated by Pete Wilson, who became governor of California. "I think there is a real sense that [Senator Feinstein] has every opportunity to make her mark," Kennedy said. "Everyone's certainly hopeful that she will."[16]

Yet along with hope there is caution, too, particularly among women in political office who know how far they still have to go to increase their numbers. Men still hold 90 percent of the seats in the U.S. Congress, 94 percent of the governors' offices, and 80 percent of the state legislative positions. Nevertheless, the women who have been elected make it easier for other women to win office. In the words of Senator Feinstein:

> As we show that women can play an articulate and effective role in the national policy debate of this country, we open doors for women. . . . We are, in effect, our sister's keeper.[17]

6

Women in High-Level
Appointed Offices

Of the top positions in the executive branch of the federal government, women have not gained parity with men. But over the past few decades, presidents have appointed an increasing number of women, including women of color, to a variety of high-level positions in the federal government. After taking office in 1993, President Clinton created one of the most diverse administrations in American history, selecting people of different age and cultural groups, as well as numerous women for top jobs.

Some of the women made history by being "firsts" in their positions, such as Janet Reno, the first woman to be appointed Attorney General. (Some highlights of her life are included in a later section.) Hazel O'Leary, who became head of the Department of Energy, is the first woman of African-American ancestry to serve in the cabinet. O'Leary took over the responsibility for a wide range of energy-producing and conservation programs as well as the nuclear weapons industry. She had previously served as a senior energy advisor in the administrations of President Gerald Ford and President Jimmy Carter. Prior to her appointment as a department head, Secretary O'Leary was the executive vice president of Northern States Power in Minneapolis, Minnesota.

Madeleine Albright, who was appointed ambassador to the United Nations, is not the first woman to hold such a position, but she is the first foreign-born member in a cabinet-level job. Her birthplace was Prague, Czechoslovakia. Albright, who once described herself as "Woman, Democrat, international affairs specialist, university professor, mother of three daughters," has been a long-time foreign policy adviser. After her appointment to the U.N. post, she noted that her family had been privileged to be part of a free America. During a press conference, she said: "You can therefore understand how proud I will be to sit at the United Nations behind the nameplate that says 'United States of America.' "[1]

Each of the women appointed in recent years could be highlighted for her accomplishments and capabilities. For example, Donna Shalala, secretary of Health and Human Services (HHS), was formerly chancellor of the University of Wisconsin at Madison and a professor of political science. During the Carter administration, she served in the Department of Housing and Urban Development. As head of HHS, Shalala is responsible for numerous duties, among them overseeing social security and welfare programs and evaluating various types of health care and new drugs.

Space permits only a few brief profiles. Nevertheless, the sketches in this chapter represent women who come from diverse backgrounds and who play important roles in government.

Justice Ginsburg

Until President Reagan appointed Sandra Day O'Connor to the U.S. Supreme Court, that body had never included a woman. Clinton's appointee, Ruth Bader Ginsburg, a federal appeals court judge, became the second woman to serve on the high court.

Born in 1933 to Jewish immigrant parents in Brooklyn, New York, Ginsburg was encouraged by her mother to be independent and to excel in school. She was considered a serious student and a scholar, graduating with honors from high school and earning top grades at Cornell University and Harvard and Columbia law schools.

Ginsburg worked hard and argued for women's civil rights during the 1960s and 1970s. She was the founding director of the Women's Rights Project of the American Civil Liberties Union, which developed legal means to eliminate sex discrimination and to protect women's rights.

During the 1970s, Ginsburg won five out of six cases concerning women's rights that she argued before the Supreme Court. This laid the groundwork for others fighting for the rights of women. In one case, Ginsburg presented a suit on behalf of Sally Reed, a divorced Idaho woman whose son had died. Both Sally Reed and her ex-husband applied to be executor of their son's estate, but Idaho law declared that the man took precedence over the woman in such cases. According to the legal reasoning, men were supposedly better able to handle business matters than women. But Ginsburg was able to show that such gender distinctions were biased. She won the case, setting a precedent for future Supreme Court decisions.

Ginsburg was a professor at Rutgers and Columbia law schools, and she also served as a judge for thirteen years before her appointment to the high court. Like other judicial appointees, she appeared before the Senate Judiciary Committee. This panel votes on whether to recommend the president's judicial appointments to the full Senate, which in turn votes to confirm or deny appointment of nominees.

During the Judiciary meetings, Ginsburg was frequently asked about her views on women's rights and whether those views would bias her decision-making. She said that judges must render decisions that are legally right, based on facts and the record. "A judge is not a politician," she said.[2]

In regard to equality for women, Ginsburg made clear that "rank discrimination is not part of our nation's culture." She also noted that a woman's right to an abortion "is something central . . . to her dignity. It's a decision that she must make for herself. And when government controls that decision for her, she's being treated as less than a fully adult human responsible for her own choices."[3]

The First Woman Attorney General

In March 1993, with her hand on a Bible held by her

fourteen-year-old niece and namesake, Janet Reno was sworn in as the United States Attorney General. She was the first woman to be appointed to the post. Prior to that time, Reno had been state attorney of Dade County, Florida. First elected in 1978, she had been re-elected for four more terms.

After her nomination as Attorney General, Reno pledged to make civil rights enforcement one of the top priorities in the Justice Department. Born in 1939, Reno, like many other professional women, has experienced sex discrimination. She was once told she could not have a job in a law office because of her gender. Later, she became a partner in that same law firm. She consistently pursued her career with the encouragement of her parents, who were both reporters. Her father died in 1966.

Jane Reno, the attorney general's mother, was a long-time guide, mentor, and heroine to Janet. From her mother, Janet said she learned integrity and how to be self-sufficient. Jane Reno, who died in 1992, was known for her pioneering spirit and was described as "a woman who wrestled alligators, drank whiskey from a coffee mug, read Proust and went rowing in hurricanes."[4] She built her own wood and stone home on the edge of the Florida Everglades, where Janet Reno lived for many years. Attorney General Reno still owns the home, which reportedly has "no air conditioning, no television, no fans, not even a washer or dryer."[5] Reno lives in the home when she is in Florida; while in Washington, D.C., she continues to maintain a frugal lifestyle.

Although she has an unassuming manner, Attorney General Reno is known by friend and foe alike as forthright. That was clear in an incident after her nomination. She was attacked personally by a Florida attorney, Jack Thompson. Thompson had long been critical of Reno and in 1988 had been her opponent for the state attorney position. He claimed that Reno was a lesbian because she had not married, trying to imply—without success—that homosexuality was a character flaw. Said Reno: "Mr. Thompson always worries about my sexual preference, but the fact is I'm just an awkward old maid with a very great affection for men."[6]

Her straightforward approach was evident in other views she expressed. On abortion, she stated simply: "I'm pro-choice." Her views on the death penalty were clear as well: "I'm personally opposed to the death penalty," she said, "but I've probably asked for it as much as any prosecutor in the country and have secured it. When the evidence and the law justify the death penalty, I will ask for it."[7]

Attorney General Reno outlined a number of other goals that she hopes to achieve. Besides civil rights, another top priority is saving America's at-risk children. A tireless advocate for children, she would like to see reforms in the juvenile justice system. In Miami, she supported an experiment to send teenagers who have committed violent crimes to an armylike boot camp for rehabilitation, which reportedly succeeded 50 percent of the time, a much better rate than for similar youth programs. She has consistently promoted treatment programs for nonviolent drug abusers and supported efforts to work with troubled children and their families as a way to stem violence.

She told *Newsweek* interviewers:

Working with dropouts at 12 and 13 is too late—they've already formed inferiority complexes. . . . We have to approach crime the way you approach parenting; you've got to have punishment that's fair, objective, that's carried out when it's threatened. You've got to let kids know that poverty, social ills of the world, are no excuse for putting a gun up against somebody's head.[8]

At the same time, Reno has promised to aggressively prosecute career criminals and place them behind bars.

Of course an attorney general has many other concerns. Reno oversees a Justice Department of more than 92,000 employees, including investigators, agents, marshals, and lawyers who are responsible for myriad law enforcement matters and legal decisions.

Certainly she has critics, and some believe that because of her gender she is not capable of handling the "top cop" job. But her supporters have called her "tough as hell." Reno considers herself a problem-solver and the "people's lawyer." In numerous interviews after her appointment, she expressed hope that she would be a force for justice and said she had no desire to be known as just a prosecutor who wins convictions.

Only time will tell whether she succeeds in her goals. But she often cites her mother's words as a motto: "You can do anything, be anything you really want to be, regardless of whether you're a woman."[9]

"Top Doc"

Another top appointee, U.S. Surgeon General Joycelyn Elders, has lived by a similar motto. She has overcome discriminatory practices against her as a woman and as a person of African-American ancestry from humble beginnings. Born in 1933, she is one of eight children of Arkansas share-croppers; her parents worked others' land and earned a share of the crops as pay. Elders spent her early years, beginning at age five, out in the field picking cotton. She has told of never being able to see a doctor until she went to college and of hearing her mother scream during difficult childbirths because no medical help was available.

In spite of her family's poverty, Elders was able to earn her degree in medicine. She became a pediatric endocrinologist (a specialist in the glands that secrete hormones) and a medical school professor. For six years she directed the Arkansas Health Department, until her 1993 confirmation as Surgeon General.

Since her tenure in Arkansas and her beginning days in Washington, D.C., Elders has been the subject of controversy. With a down-to-earth style, she has spoken out in no uncertain terms about major public health problems, such as the epidemic of teenage pregnancies and family violence. Her supporters have characterized her as "forceful" and a "fearless crusader," while opponents call her a "publicity-hungry radical." In the words of one supporter, Elders "is a diamond in the rough—her opponents see the rough, but they always miss the diamond."[10]

One issue that she feels "very strongly about is that every child born in America be a planned, wanted child." She has long advocated providing health services for and contraception information—including making condoms available—to young people. In Elders' view, preventive health services are "primary" and could help reduce poverty, substance abuse, sexually transmitted diseases, and other social problems. She would like to see comprehensive health education become a part of America's schools. "You can't educate children if they aren't healthy, and you can't keep them healthy if they aren't educated," she said during one interview.[11]

Many who oppose contraception and Elders' views on abortion have criticized her for not trying to discourage behavior that leads to unwanted pregnancies and sexual diseases. Opponents also have called Elders "bigoted" and "intolerant" because of her past critical statements on the position of the Catholic Church and the "Bible-belt" in denouncing family planning and abortion.

Still, Elders' straight talk has made sense even to those who have had reservations about her views. In her testimony before the confirmation committee, she said bluntly:

> I have seen bright young people all over this country in an ocean surrounded by the sharks of drugs, alcohol, violence, homicide, suicide, AIDS, and teenage pregnancy while we argue over whose values we are going to teach.[12]

In the end, she was confirmed by a 65 to 34 vote, with some senators previously in opposition admitting that Elders was issuing a "wake-up call" to the country. Nancy Kassebaum, one of the few Republicans who voted for Elders' confirmation, put it this way: "She [Elders] can reach an audience of younger people that I could never reach."[13]

Role of the First Lady

Although not appointed to an established position in the federal government, the first lady, wife of the president, plays an important role in the nation's political life. When Hillary Rodham Clinton became first lady, the media seemed obsessed with what her role would be, asking: How much clout will she have? What should her title be? Is she a new breed of first lady? Should she play a prominent role in government? Should the president seek her advice? Will she be too powerful?

The questions were posed, and superficial attempts were made to answer them because Hillary Rodham Clinton was not only first lady but also a partner with her husband in decision-making. Early in his administration, President Clinton asked his wife to head up a task force that would recommend ways to make health care more affordable and available for Americans.

To some of the public, First Lady Hillary Rodham Clinton seemed to be acting as copresident, and critics charged that she had not been elected to make decisions or give advice. Yet every president accepts advice from nonelected officials, for example, those appointed to office and hired staff. Many have also sought suggestions and opinions from their wives.

By all accounts, the first lady is a skilled, accomplished attorney. The *National Law Journal* twice named her one of "The 100 Most Influential Lawyers in America." Nationally recognized as an advocate for children's rights, she served for years on the board of the Children's Defense Fund, an advocacy organization. She has also supported worker training programs and affordable housing for low-income people.

But over the years, many Americans have been uneasy about the possibility of a first lady who might break some of the unspoken and unwritten rules for presidents' wives. Most of the first ladies in the United States have been "silent partners," seen-but-not-heard helpmates who serve as hostesses but essentially withdraw from public life. Or they have taken on what the public has perceived as women's political or public welfare interests—for example, Barbara Bush choosing to be a symbolic spokeswoman for literacy programs. When they have departed from the historical and traditional role, first ladies have been widely and often cruelly criticized, as was Eleanor Roosevelt.

During the 1930s, when her husband Franklin Roosevelt was president, Eleanor Roosevelt crusaded tirelessly to try to rectify some of the social ills of the time, working in particular to help the many unemployed and poor who barely had the basic necessities to survive. In newspaper columns, on the radio, and in public speeches she championed civil rights, called for decent and affordable housing with indoor plumbing for all Americans, and supported many efforts to provide funds for broad-based health care and public education. But many news reporters, cartoonists, and political opponents mercilessly attacked her and her efforts. She was accused of everything from "wearing the pants in the family" to being a communist. Nevertheless, she refused to back down, continued to be part of the political scene, and urged other women to become political activists.

Eleanor Roosevelt has been an ideal for women in many walks of life, and Hillary Rodham Clinton has frequently cited her admiration for Roosevelt's activism. While the public frets and stews over the role of first ladies, there is little doubt that the first lady has tried to take control of her own life and define herself, rather than allowing others to do so. Perhaps she will be seen in the future as another type of model for women—a first lady who takes a leadership role in government and is an influence for the public good.

Winning State and Local Offices

As women have achieved high-profile positions in federal government and have gained in United States congressional seats, they have also won an increasing number of seats in state legislatures. According to the Center for the American Woman and Politics at Rutgers, women made up 20.5 percent of state legislators across the United States in 1993, a steady increase from 1969 when women were only 4 percent of state senators and representatives. Washington had the largest percentage—39.5 percent of the state's legislature was female in 1993—and Alabama and Kentucky were at the bottom of the list. (See chart on pages 98-99.)

Women also are increasing their numbers in such state offices as attorney general and secretary of state. Voters in conservative and traditional Indiana, for example, chose two women in 1992 to serve in major elective

WOMEN IN STATE LEGISLATURES 1993

State	State Rank	Senate		Total Women/Total Senate	House		Total Women/Total House	Total Women/Total Legis.	% Women Overall
		D	R		D	R			
AK	49	1	1	2/35	5	0	5/105	7/140	5.0
AL	21	3	1	4/20	5	4	9/40	13/60	21.7
AZ	2	3	6	9/30	9	14	23/60	32/90	35.6
AR	46	1	0	1/35	10	2	12/100	13/135	9.6
CA	18	2	3^	6/40	18	4	22/80	28/120	23.3
CO	3	3	5	8/35	16	11	27/65	35/100	35.0
CT	13	4	4	8/36	27	12	39/151	47/187	25.1
DE	38	2	1	3/21	2	4	6/41	9/62	14.5
FL	31	4	2	6/40	16	6	22/120	28/160	17.5
GA	32	4	2	6/56	23	12	35/180	41/236	17.4
HI	17	5	1	6/25	10	2	12/51	18/76	23.7
ID	7	6	3	9/35	6	17	23/70	32/105	30.5
IL	19	5	6	11/59	15	15	30/118	41/177	23.2
IN	28	7	6	13/50	7	9	16/100	29/150	19.3
IA	37	4	2	6/50	8	8	16/100	22/150	14.7
KS	8	3	11	14/40	19	15	34/125	48/165	29.1
KY	50	1	0	1/38	3	2	5/100	6/138	4.3
LA	48	1	0	1/39	8	2	10/105	11/144	7.6
ME	6	7	4	11/35	36	12	48/151	59/186	31.7
MD	16	10	0	10/47	30	5	35/141	45/188	23.9
MA	20	7	2	9/40	25	12	37/160	46/200	23.0
MI	24	2	1	3/38	15	12	27/110	30/148	20.3
MN	10	12	8	20/67	25	10	35/134	55/201	27.4
MS	44	3	1	4/52	13	2	15/122	19/174	10.9
MO	29	0	1	1/34	22	14	36/163	37/197	18.8
MT	25+	7	2	9/50	13	8	21/100	30/150	20.0

WOMEN IN STATE LEGISLATURES 1993

State	State Rank	Senate D	Senate R	Total Women/Total Senate	House D	House R	Total Women/Total House	Total Women/Total Legis.	% Women Overall
NE	23	Nonpartisan		10/49	Unicameral			10/49	20.4
NV	12	3	2	5/21	9	3	12/42	17/63	27.0
NH	5	6	3	9/24	59	74	133/400	142/424	33.5
NJ	41	1	0	1/40	2	12	14/80	15/120	12.5
NM	27	6	2	8/42	9	5	14/70	22/112	19.6
NY	33	7	1	8/61	21	6	27/150	35/211	16.6
NC	30	6	1	7/50	15	9	24/120	31/170	18.2
ND	35	5	3	8/49	8	8	16/98	24/147	16.3
OH	22	1	4	5/33	13	10	23/99	28/132	21.2
OK	47	5	1	6/48	5	3	8/101	14/149	9.4
OR	9	7	1	8/30	11	6	17/60	25/90	27.8
PA	45	3	1	4/50	11	10	21/203	25/253	9.9
RI	14	9	2	11/50	18	8	26/100	37/150	24.7
SC	40	2	1	3/46	10	9	19/124	22/170	12.9
SD	25+	6	1	7/35	3	11	14/70	21/105	20.0
TN	43	2	1	3/33	8	5	13/99	16/132	12.1
TX	36	2	2	4/31	18	7	25/150	29/181	16.0
UT	39	1	1	2/29	4	8	12/75	14/104	13.5
VT	4	7	4	11/30	34	16	50/150	61/180	33.9
VA	42	3	1	4/40	10	3	13/100	17/140	12.1
WA	1	14	4	18/49	26	14	40/98	58/147	39.5
WV	34	4	1	5/34	14	3	17/100	22/134	16.4
WI	11	2	7	9/33	16	11	27/99	36/132	27.3
WY	15	1	4	5/30	6	11	17/60	22/90	24.4
Total		210	121	342/1,984	716	466	1,182/5,440	1,524/7,424	20.5

+States with the same *exact* percentage (MT & SD) are given the same rank. States which round out to the same figure (TN & VA), but are not exactly the same, are ranked differently.
^ Indicates an additional independent member in the California Senate.

offices in the statehouse, bringing the number of women to four out of a total of eight such positions. Of those women, Pam Carter was the first African-American woman to be elected to a state attorney general office and the first woman to hold such a position in Indiana.

Ever-larger numbers of women have won election to local school boards, city councils, and many other government offices. For some women, winning a state or local office lays the foundation for a higher position in federal government. For others, it is simply a way to be involved in politics and to have a voice in the kind of governing that has the most direct impact on their community and their own lives.

Women as Mayors

Over the years, women have been able to win more elected offices at the local level of government than at the state or national levels. America's first woman mayor was 27-year-old Susanna Medora Salter who was elected in 1887 in Argonia, Kansas, even though she did not know her name was on the ballot. The Woman's Christian Temperance Union submitted her name, and two-thirds of the voters elected her. However, she served for only one year, receiving a salary of one dollar.

Ophelia "Birdie" Harwood was another mayor who was elected even before women had the right to vote. A strong-willed woman on the frontier, Harwood became mayor of Marble Falls, Texas, near Houston in 1917. She died in 1954 and was only recently honored by the city for her early role in government.

During the 1940s through the 1960s, women became

increasingly visible in elected local offices. An example was Margaret Prickett, a businesswoman who in 1964 became mayor of Mishawaka, Indiana, a medium-sized town in the northern part of the state. Mayor Prickett was the first woman to serve as mayor of the town and set a precedent for other women in neighboring cities and throughout the state to follow.

Known for her many different hats, Prickett wore a fancy hat—flowered, wide-brimmed, furry, or beribboned—for every ceremonial occasion. She used her trademark to her advantage when she was invited to her first civic dinner that traditionally had been a male-only affair. Mayor Prickett knew that the men planning the dinner were concerned about inviting her since she would be the only woman present. So to ease their fears, she sent her "agent."

Carefully, she placed her fanciest hat in a box, called a taxi, and ordered the driver to take the box to the dinner. The hat was put on the table at the place set for the mayor. Although the hat became the "guest" at that dinner, it and the mayor's sense of humor helped break the male resistance to Prickett taking her place as the city's boss.

Although women have won mayoral offices throughout the century, it was not until the beginning of the 1980s that women were elected in any substantial numbers to serve as mayors of big and medium-sized cities. From 1979 to 1983, Jane Byrne held the top administrative job in Chicago, the largest city yet to elect a woman for mayor. Other large cities headed by women during the 1980s include Charlotte, North Carolina; Dallas, Texas; Honolulu, Hawaii; Little Rock, Arkansas; San

Francisco, California; Richmond, Virginia; St. Petersburg, Florida; and Spokane, Washington.

In the 1992 elections, women won mayoral offices in a variety of towns and cities across the United States. To cite a few examples: several towns in Florida elected female mayors for the first time; in East Point, Atlanta, Patsy Jo Hilliard became the first African-American woman mayor of that suburban community; Ruth Bascom ushered in a new political era in Eugene, Oregon, as the first woman to serve as the city's mayor. Women were also elected to mayoral positions in several Missouri and Pennsylvania towns.

In suburban communities north and west of Chicago, at least seventeen women were in the top positions. Similarly, in Santa Clara County, California, women have held top jobs in local government for some time, but after the 1992 elections, eight out of fifteen cities in the county were headed by women as mayors—a new achievement.

According to Mary Hornbuckle, mayor of Costa Mesa, California, women spoke out and took "more assertive roles" in 1992 than in past election years. She said:

> I think it's very important that we have both men and women's voices heard and recognized in the governmental process. The successes that women had in being elected to the Senate certainly should be encouraging to anyone following in their footsteps. And I'm encouraged when I see cities throughout the country electing women mayors and women to their city councils.[1]

Recent efforts to put women in local offices have

been spearheaded by women's political groups that want to see women seated across a broad spectrum of government, from local councils to mayor to governor. At the same time, many voters have been convinced that women candidates are dedicated and committed to their communities and are hard-working advocates for such local concerns as quality education. Voters also have seen women as caring individuals with a sense of responsibility.

Those characteristics were cited as reasons a Missouri woman, Linda Givens, was elected in 1993 to be mayor of Pine Lawn, a suburb of St. Louis, Missouri. Givens is also a junior high school teacher. As the first woman mayor of the town, she has the support of not only adults in the community but also the backing of her students. One seventh-grader said she is "really organized, like a mayor should be." Another said Givens is "willing to take responsibility for things she does. She really cares about us, and it shows."[2]

Mayoral elections were held in a number of major cities in the fall of 1993, and women were prominent candidates in such cities as Atlanta, Boston, Detroit, and Minneapolis. However, the only woman to win in a metropolitan center was Sharon Sayles Belton of Minneapolis, the former president of the City Council. Her election marked two historical feats: she is the first person of African-American ancestry and the first woman to serve as a mayor of Minneapolis.

Voters saw Sayles Belton as independent—her own person—and believed she was capable of bringing people of diverse backgrounds together. An editorial in the metropolitan daily newspaper called her election proof of "healthful social changes" that have taken place in the city because of advocates for "a more inclusive society." The editorial also praised Sayles Belton's victory as a "latter-day American success story," describing her as

> A child of divorce, abandoned by the father of her disabled eldest child while still in college, Sayles Belton responded to difficult circumstances not with despair but with determination. Her belief that government must help cultivate the resources, internal and external, for other young people at a challenging crossroads has sturdy roots in her own experience.[3]

Year of the Woman Governor?

"1994—The Year of the Woman Governor." Women's political groups began using that theme right after the 1992 elections, signaling a strategy to elect women to the top administrative post in a number of states. Women in politics reason that a governorship is a particularly good platform from which a woman can seek a candidacy for president of the United States. Presidents Ronald Reagan and Bill Clinton were former governors and as a result gained political support and financial backing for their successful presidential races.

The first woman governor, Nellie Tayloe Ross, served in Wyoming from 1925 to 1927, completing the term of her deceased husband. Since that time, a total of twelve women have held governorships, with eight elected to office in their own right.

Most of the women who have campaigned for governorships in the 1990s have brought a variety of political experiences to their campaigns. They have laid groundwork over many years of political activism, and most have held elected state or local government offices.

However, as in other political races today, a candidate for governor, whether female or male, usually has to be seen by voters as an agent of change and free of influence by those seeking special favors. In the view of Celinda Lake, a Democratic pollster, and Linda DiVall, a Republican pollster, women candidates who appear credible and challenge incumbents have a good chance of winning in future elections.

In an editorial piece for *USA Today,* the two pollsters cited the 1993 election of Christine Todd Whitman. According to Lake and DiVall, the newly elected New Jersey governor "overcame a very poor campaign in part because she was not the incumbent." She also was able to convince voters that she was committed to her campaign pledges. On the other hand, in Virginia, candidate Mary Sue Terry, "who started out as a voice for change, was beaten in part because she was seen as a 'pseudo-incumbent.' " Terry had served two terms as the state's attorney general.

As has been true for many years, one of the drawbacks for women running for the top position in a state (and also for a mayoral position) is that "voters are more cautious about electing women to executive posts than legislative posts." Why? Because as many women candidates have pointed out and the pollsters have confirmed: "Overall, voters believe women . . . are better listeners and work better at negotiations—all legislative traits." But they think women are not as capable as men in the executive positions "in handling crises, supervising big budgets and staffs, being tough and managing," according to the surveys that both Democrats and Republicans conducted during 1992.[4]

Most women candidates for executive positions well understand the stereotypes that they have to overcome and the fine balancing act that they have to perform. As Lake and DiVall described the situation:

> Voters worry first and foremost whether women will be tough enough to be governors, yet they also feel uncomfortable when women come across as too tough. A female candidate, in a time of crisis during a campaign or in her incumbency, needs to speak out for herself, show calmness and demonstrate command of the facts."[5]

A Popular Governor

Speaking out for herself and straight talk in general have been part of Texas Governor Ann Richards' style since she entered politics in 1975, winning the office of Travis County commissioner and then later being elected to the state treasurer's office. She became widely known for her warmth, humor, and biting comments after her keynote address to the Democratic convention of 1988, when she described Republican presidential candidate George Bush as the fellow "born with a silver foot in his mouth."

More characteristic of Richards' honest, open manner, however, has been her public discussion of past personal difficulties. During her campaign for the governorship in 1990, reporters asked probing questions about the breakup of her thirty-year marriage and her battle with alcoholism. In her responses, Richards described her divorce as one of the most painful parts of her life. She saw it as a failure, but a failure that she was able to overcome by learning that she could live alone and be content with herself.

Admitting to alcoholism could have brought public censure and enough negative criticism to destroy any political career. But Richards was able to point out the positive side: that she sought treatment through Alcoholics Anonymous and became a recovering alcoholic. She has been sober since 1980. By speaking frankly about her disease, Richards was able to show that it is possible to get through difficult times and rectify past mistakes.

Certainly, being able to deal in a positive and bold manner with adversity is a trait that has helped Ann Richards build a political career, particularly in a state known for its hard-driving, hard-hitting male dominance. Another helpful trait has been her ability to project a caring attitude and down-home, country charm along with wit and wisdom. Like many other women in politics, she also has been able to show toughness when needed. As one political writer described her:

> Richards is more complicated than she seems. So appealing is her famously warm, humorous good-ol'-girl persona that it is tempting to look no further. But . . . Richards' personal and political history have made her fiercely wary and, when need be, as tough as boiled owl.[6]

However people view her, Richards has been one of the most popular governors in the nation. "She's our idol," is how two Houston teenagers described their governor recently.

8

Unfinished Business

Will women be able to bridge the gender gap that still exists in public life and in many other areas of power? Will the Equal Rights Amendment pass? Will more women continue to run for governmental offices? Will a woman be elected president of the United States?

These are just a few of the questions posed in regard to the unfinished business of women in politics. While there are many conflicting views on what the future will hold for women and their search for equity, there is consensus that women will not be silenced. They will continue to speak out on issues important to them, not the least of which is the Equal Rights Amendment.

The Equal Rights Amendment

In 1972, Congress passed the proposed twenty-seventh amendment to the U.S. Constitution known as the

Equal Rights Amendment (ERA). As required by the U.S. Constitution, the proposed amendment was submitted to the states for ratification. Congress set the ratification deadline for March 1979, then extended it to June 30, 1982. Although the amendment was supported by Democrat and Republican presidents and by many officeholders of both parties, only thirty-five state legislatures voted to ratify it by the deadline. Three-fourths of the states—thirty-eight total—must ratify an amendment before it can be part of the constitution.

Eleanor Smeal, head of the Fund for the Feminist Majority and former president of NOW, noted that "Throughout the 1970s, there seemed to be little difference between the parties on women's issues." But by the early 1980s, the "New Right" wing of the Republican party—people who believe that men should dominate in politics and all aspects of society—began to oppose not only the ERA but also abortion and affirmative action for women and people of color in employment and education. According to Smeal, the conservatives organized those who feared change and fought to preserve white male supremacy. Smeal wrote in the 1980s that:

> The New Right represented itself as the anointed custodian not only of superpatriotism and the flag, but of the American family as well. All equitable changes sought for women became an attack on the family. In the New Right's view, nothing could be allowed to interfere with a man's right to dominate his family. Not only legislation designed to protect battered wives but child-abuse legislation designed to protect abused children was attacked as "antifamily."[1]

Indeed, the right-wing attacks against the ERA were and still are highly organized. Ironically, women who have joined the opposition have been politicized—motivated by a feeling of empowerment and, like their opponents, using the political process to fight for causes they believe in.

One of the most militant political groups, Stop ERA, has been led by Phyllis Schafly who has consistently argued that women biologically are not equal to men and that the ERA would destroy social institutions like marriage and the family. She and others who share her view also contend that there is adequate legal protection for the rights of women and no other protective laws are needed. Schafly has often declared that women should value the privileges they have and stick to old traditions, staying in the home and caring for children, although she herself has long traveled nationwide, speaking and organizing.

Although the ERA was reintroduced in Congress, it has not been approved. Over the years some states have included the principles outlined in the ERA in their constitutions or passed state ERAs. Efforts to pass equal rights laws at the state level also have continued. In 1992, for example, the ERA was on the ballot in Iowa. It appeared at first that voters would support it, but the amendment was defeated by a narrow margin: 52 percent to 48 percent.

Opponents of ERA in Iowa argued that passing the amendment would result in the loss of many benefits for women and would allow tax funds to be used for abortions. Opponents also claimed that homosexuals would receive special rights if ERA passed.

Women's rights advocates accused ERA opponents, particularly the Stop ERA movement, of using scare tactics and lies in their Iowa campaign. ERA supporters also said they were slow to respond to negative attacks and that the news media in Iowa seldom questioned the truth of anti-ERA statements.

Carrying on the Fight

There is little doubt that the fight for the ERA will continue, since numerous polls show that the majority of Americans support the amendment. But many other issues that concern women must be tackled in the future. In addition, women in politics know that they have to educate the general public on the fact that what affects a woman in adverse ways can have a harmful impact on those around her. And when half the population is excluded from positions of economic and political power, the total society can suffer. A community, state, or nation loses the contributions that women can make.

Neil Chethik, who writes the "Men's Column" for the *Detroit Free Press,* pointed out that the male grip on power in our total society has been damaging to both men and women. Men pay for it in stress-related illness and shortened life spans. Power struggles also frequently end in violent deaths. And men lose out on opportunities to relate to women on an equal basis, thus "men's personal and professional relationships with women are tainted by anger and mistrust," Chethik wrote. In his view:

> [there will be no easy] transition from men holding power to women and men sharing power. . . .

Women have had different experiences, and they bring a new and often challenging perspective to leadership. But if men can allow themselves to be challenged, if we can listen openly to women and respond with respect for both women and ourselves, then both genders can benefit equally from the changes ahead."[2]

Of course many men *can* "listen openly," and over the past decade or so men from a wide range of backgrounds have acknowledged women's valuable role in government. The public in general also has given more credence and attention to women's concerns, as was evident in 1993 when Congress passed a record number of laws—at least thirty—that benefit women and children.

Yet the changes go beyond public perceptions and beneficial laws. In increasing numbers, women themselves have become more assertive and have found ways to be heard and respected for what they do. U.S. Representative Nancy Johnson from Connecticut, a state with many politically active women, stated the case for women in politics succinctly: "We didn't get to where we are because we are women. We got there because we're capable leaders."[3]

Chapter Notes

Chapter 1

1. Quoted in Ronald Brownstein, "Women Gather to Plan Further Political Gains," *Los Angeles Times* (July 9, 1993), B1.

2. Personal interview, February 1992.

Chapter 2

1. Quoted in Frank Donovan, ed., *The John Adams Papers* (New York: Dodd, Mead, 1965), p. 55.

2. Ibid.

3. Ibid., p. 59.

4. Ibid., p. 60.

5. Quoted in Eleanor Flexner, *Century of Struggle: The Woman's Rights Movement in the United States* (New York: Atheneum, 1974), p. 47.

6. Ibid., pp. 74–76.

7. Quoted in Marie Hecht, Joan D. Berbrich, Sally Healey, and Clare Cooper, *The Women, Yes* (New York: Holt, Rinehart and Winston, 1973), pp. 65–68.

8. Flexner, p. 69.

9. Quoted in Margaret Washington, ed., *Narrative of Sojourner Truth* (New York: Vintage Books/Random House, 1993), p. 118.

10. Flexner, p. 60.

11. Ibid., pp. 188–189.

Chapter 3

1. Harriett Woods, "Opportunities Amid the Anger," *The National Voter* (June/July 1992), p. 21.

2. Quoted in Paul Houston, "Washington Insight," *Los Angeles Times* (June 21, 1993), p. A5.

3. Quoted in Toni Locy, "A Lesson for Women for '92 Fund-Raisers' Merger Spurs Hope for Political Success," *Boston Globe* (May 4, 1993), Metro section, p. 21.

4. William J. Eaton, "Control of Senate at Stake as 10 Races Go Down to Wire," *Los Angeles Times* (October 30, 1992), p. A13.

5. Quoted in Marla Williams and Robert T. Nelson, "Murray Wins Key Appointment," *Seattle Times* (January 7, 1993), p. G1.

6. "Serving the Country," *USA Today* (September 24, 1992), News section, p. 1A.

7. "Battle of the Sexes," *Psychology Today* (September/October 1992), p. 13.

8. Dorothy W. Cantor and Toni Bernay, with Jean Stoess, *Women in Power: The Secrets of Leadership* (Boston: Houghton Mifflin, 1992), p. 75.

9. "Women Candidates Scanty Coverage," *Psychology Today* (July/August 1992), p. 12.

10. Quoted in Carol Bergman, "The Lady is a Pol," *Cosmopolitan* (January 1992), p. 159.

11. Locy, p. 21.

12. Cantor, Bernay, and Stoess, p. 83.

13. Lynn Yeakel, "Campaign Finance Reform," *Philadelphia Inquirer* (May 29, 1993), p. A11.

14. Jon Friedman, "Ms. Kingmaker," *San Francisco Chronicle* (May 16, 1993), section Z1, p. 11.

15. Friedman, p. 11.

16. Statement of Representative Lynn C. Woolsey at press conference, June 15, 1993.

Chapter 4

1. Gail Collins, "Potty Politics: The Gender Gap," *Working Woman* (March 1993), p. 93.

2. Quoted in Michael Ross, "11 New Senators Get Briefing on Rules—Including Ones They Vowed to Break," *Los Angeles Times* (November 10, 1992), p. A22.

3. "Larry King Live," CNN, November 10, 1992.

4. "Equal Time," CNBC, July 20, 1993.

5. Quoted in Claude Lewis, "Two Congresswomen Roughed Up Before the 103rd Congress Begins," *Philadelphia Inquirer* (January 6, 1993), p. A7.

6. Quoted in Nelda LaTeef, *Working Women for the 21st Century: 50 Women Reveal Their Pathways to Career Success* (Charlotte, Vt: Williamson Publishing, 1992), p. 208.

7. Phone interview with Kassebaum aides, June 1993.

8. Quoted in Kerry O'Rourke, "Mikulski Pays Visit, Hears Local Concerns," *Baltimore Morning Sun* (February 10, 1993), p. 5B.

9. Quoted in Roger K. Lowe, "Freshmen Shaking Foundations of House with Surprising Force," *The Columbus Dispatch* (March 28, 1993), p. 2A.

10. Quoted in Nena Baker, "First Things Furse," *The Oregonian* (May 30, 1993), p. L5.

Chapter 5

1. Quoted in Geraldine Baum, "Knocking at the Door," *Los Angeles Times* (December 29, 1992), p. E1.

2. Quoted in Stephen Gascoyne, "Pat Schroeder Targets Gender Barriers," *Christian Science Monitor* (August 27, 1992), p. 7.

3. Quoted in Rosemary Dempsey, "NOW Lobby Day Success," *National Times* (April 1993), p. 2.

4. Statement of Senator Patty Murray on Family and

Medical Leave Act on the floor of the U.S. Senate, February 2, 1993.

5. "Boxer Says Women Making Mark in Senate," *San Francisco Chronicle* (July 12, 1993), p. A2.

6. "The Ovarian Cancer Research Act of 1991," *Congressional Record,* Vol. 137, No. 32, February 26, 1991.

7. Statement by U.S. Representative Patsy T. Mink before the Appropriations Subcommittee on Labor, Health and Human Services and Education, May 19, 1992.

8. Marcia Angell, "Caring for Women's Health: What Is the Problem?" *The New England Journal of Medicine* (July 22, 1993), pp. 271–272.

9. Remarks of Congresswoman Rosa L. DeLauro, First Annual Congress on Women's Health, June 4, 1993.

10. Ibid.

11. Lini S. Kadaba, "Women Are Still in Working Ghetto," St. Louis Post-Dispatch (July 14, 1993), p. 3F.

12. Representative Deborah Pryce, "Congress Must Get Tough on Crimes Against Women," press release, June 22, 1993.

13. Congresswoman Maxine Waters, "An Urban Agenda for America," speech on the floor of the House of Representatives, January 27, 1993.

14. Ibid.

15. Robert T. Nelson, "Delegation Supports Bill to Reinstate Ban on Export of Logs," *Seattle Times* (June 8, 1993), p. B2.

16. Quoted in Glenn F. Bunting, "Feinstein Takes Oath as U.S. Senator," *Los Angeles Times* (November 11, 1992), p. A3.

17. "Feinstein Lauds Women's New Political Power," *San Francisco Chronicle* (July 10, 1993), p. A2.

Chapter 6

1. Quoted in Robert C. Toth, "U.N. Appointee's 'American Story,'" *Los Angeles Times* (December 23, 1992), p. A18.

2. Quoted in Joan Biskupic, "Ginsburg Hearings Elicit Sketchy View," *The Washington Post* (July 26, 1993), p A6.

3. Ibid.

4. Mitchell Landsberg, Associated Press news story, February 14, 1993.

5. Mike Clary, "Modest Reno Is Not the Typical Capital Insider," *Los Angeles Times* (February 13, 1993), p. A1.

6. Quoted in Clary, p. A20.

7. Quoted in David Lauter, "Miami Prosecutor Is Atty. Gen. Choice," *Los Angeles Times* (February 12, 1993), pp. A1, A14.

8. Melinda Liu and Bob Cohn, "The Reluctant Star," *Newsweek* (May 17, 1993), p. 43.

9. Quoted in Barbara Gordon, "Will She Be A Force for Change?" *Parade Magazine* (May 2, 1993), p. 5.

10. Quoted in Helen Dewar, "Elders Is Confirmed as Surgeon General," *The Washington Post* (September 8, 1993), p. A4.

11. Quoted in Marlene Cimons, "Elders Calls Education the Best Rx," *Los Angeles Times* (December 24, 1992), p. A5.

12. Quoted in John Schwartz, "Elders Ends Silence Before Senate Panel," *The Washington Post* (July 24, 1993), p. A8.

13. Quoted in John Schwartz, "Senate Panel Backs Elders," *The Washington Post* (July 31, 1993), p. A1.

Chapter 7

1. Mary Hornbuckle, "Woman's Place," *Los Angeles Times* (November 24, 1992), p. B11.

2. Quoted in Lia Nower, "New Mayor Plans to Tackle Job with Energy," *St. Louis Post-Dispatch* (April 19, 1993), p. 1.

3. "Minneapolis Mayor Race Belton Win Is Sign of Healthful Change," *St. Paul Pioneer Press* (November 3, 1993), editorial, p. 14A.

4. Celinda Lake and Linda DiVall, "Voter Cynicism Is Boon for Women," *USA Today* (November 18, 1993), p. 15A.

5. Ibid.

6. Alison Cook, "Lone Star," *New York Times Magazine* (February 7, 1993), p. 27.

Chapter 8

1. Eleanor Smeal, *Why and How Women Will Elect the Next President* (New York: Harper & Row, 1984), p. 81.

2. Neil Chethik. "It's a Deadly Mistake for Men to Hoard Power," *Detroit Free Press* (March 14, 1993), p. 2J.

3. Quoted in Elizabeth Ross, "Connecticut's Powerful Women," *Christian Science Monitor* (May 3, 1993), p. 14.

Further Reading

Cantor, Dorothy W. and Toni Bernay, with Jean Stoess. *Women in Power: The Secrets of Leadership.* Boston: Houghton Mifflin, 1992.

Davis, Flora. *Moving the Mountain: The Women's Movement in America since 1960.* New York: Simon & Schuster, 1991.

Dee, Catherine. *Women's Political Action Guide.* Berkeley, Calif.: Earth Works, 1993.

Fannon, Cecilia. *Leaders* (Women Today Series). Vero Beach, Fla.: Rourke Publishing Group, 1991.

Flexner, Eleanor. *Century of Struggle: The Woman's Rights Movement in the United States.* New York: Atheneum, 1974.

Garner, Cindy. *If Women Ran Things.* Austin, Tex.: Newport House, 1993.

Lansing, Jewel. *Campaigning for Office: A Woman Runs.* Saratoga, Calif.: R & E Publishers, 1991.

Lee, Richard S. and Mary Price Lee. *Careers for Women in Politics.* New York: Rosen Publishing Group, 1989.

Marcy, Samuel J. *Equal and Distinct Genders: Representation of Women by Women & Men by Men.* Fort Collins, Colo.: EJUT Books, 1993.

Morris, Celia. *Storming the Statehouse: Running for Governor with Ann Richards and Dianne Feinstein.* New York: Macmillan, 1992.

Mulford, Carolyn. *Elizabeth Dole: Public Servant* (Contemporary Women Series). Hillside, N.J.: Enslow Publishers, 1992.

Rajoppi, Joanne. *Women in Office: Getting There and Staying There.* Westport, Conn.: Greenwood, 1993.

Schneider, Carl, and Dorothy Schneider. *American Women in the Progressive Era.* New York: Facts on File, 1992.

Stephenson, June. *Women's Roots.* Napa, Calif.: Diemer, Smith Publishing, 1981.

Theilmann, John. *Discrimination and Congressional Campaign Contributions.* Westport, Conn.: Greenwood, *1991.*

Where to Write For More Information

American Association of University Women, 1111 16th Street, N.W., Washington, DC 20036

Capitol Hill Women's Political Caucus, Longworth House Office Building, P.O. Box 599, Washington, DC 20515

Catholic Women for the ERA, 1036 Enquirer Building, 617 Vine Street, Cincinnati, OH 45202

Center for the American Woman and Politics, Eagleton Institute of Politics, 90 Clifton Avenue, Rutgers University, New Brunswick, NJ 08903

Center for Responsive Governance, 1000 16th Street, N.W., Suite 500, Washington, DC 20036

Center for Women Policy Studies, 2000 P Street, N.W., Suite 508, Washington, DC 20036

Clearinghouse on Women's Issues, P.O. Box 70603, Friendship Heights, MD 20813

Congressional Caucus for Women's Issues, 2471 Rayburn Office Building, Washington, DC 20515

Council of State Governments, 444 North Capitol Street, Washington, DC 20001

EMILY's List, 1112 16th Street, N.W., Suite 750, Washington, DC 20036

Fund for the Feminist Majority, 1600 Wilson Boulevard, No. 801, Arlington, VA 22209

Joint Center for Political and Economic Studies, 1090 Vermont Avenue, N.W., Suite 1100, Washington, DC 20005

League of Women Voters of the United States, 1730 M
Street, N.W., Washington, DC 20036

MS. Foundation for Women, 141 Fifth Avenue, Suite 6-5,
New York, NY 10010

National Black Women's Political Leadership Caucus, 3005
Blandensburg Road, N.E., No. 217, Washington, DC
20018

National Council of Women of the United States, 777 United
Nations Plaza, New York, NY 10017

National Organization for Women, 1000 16th Street, N.W.,
Washington, DC 20036

National Women's Political Caucus, 1275 K Street, N.W.,
No. 750, Washington, DC 20005

Religious Network for Equality for Women, 475 Riverside
Drive, Room A12-A, New York, NY 10115

United States House of Representatives, Washington, DC
20515

United States Senate, Washington, DC 20510

WISH List, 210 West Front Street, Red Bank, NJ 07701

Women's Campaign Fund, 120 Maryland Avenue, N.E.,
Washington, DC 20002

Women's Leadership Network, Box 7412, Fairfax Station, VA
22039

Women's Rights Project, c/o American Civil Liberties Union,
132 West 43rd Street, New York, NY 10036

Index

A

abolition, 17, 19–20, 22, 27
abortion(s), 37, 42, 65, 66,
    68–70, 88, 90, 93, 110,
    111
Abzug, Bella, 50
Adams, Abigail, 18
Adams, John, 17, 18, 19
Addams, Jane, 24
African Americans, 42, 49, 60,
    85, 92, 100, 102
Alabama, 97
Albright, Madeline, 14, 86
American Anti-Slavery Society,
    20
American Civil Liberties
    Union, 24, 87
*American Slavery As It Is:
    Testimony of a Thousand
    Witnesses*, 20
American Woman Suffrage
    Association, 28–29, 31
Anthony, Susan B., 26–27
Arizona, 50
Arkansas, 92, 101
attorney general
    state, 97, 100, 105
    United States. *See* Reno,
    Janet.

B

Bagley, Sarah, 24–25
Bascom, Mayor Ruth, 102
Bentsen, Lloyd, 8
Black Caucus, 60

Blackwell, Elizabeth, 24
Boergers, Mary, 10
Boxer, Senator Barbara, 50, 52,
    71–72
Browner, Carol, 14
Bush, Barbara, 95
Bush, President George, 14, 70,
    106
Byrne, Jane, 101

C

cabinet members, 14
California, 10, 44, 55, 60, 78,
    80, 83, 102
campaign(s), 7, 32–33, 38–42,
    44, 54, 104–106, 112
Campbell, Senator Ben
    Nighthorse, 52
Cantwell, Congresswoman
    Maria, 62
Carter, President Jimmy, 86
Carter, State Attorney General
    Pam, 100
Center for the American
    Woman and Politics, 32,
    97
Chisholm, Shirley, 32
Ciller, Prime Minister Tansu,
    11
Civil War, 27, 52
Clayton, Congresswoman Eva,
    49
Clinton, Hillary Rodham, 94–96
Clinton, President Bill, 14, 85,
    87, 104

Collins, Congresswoman
    Cardiss, 60
Colorado, 28, 45, 52
Congressional Caucus for
    Women's Issues, 66, 73
Connecticut, 73, 113
Continental Congress, 18
Council of Economic Advisors,
    14
Czechoslovakia, 86

D
"Decade of the Woman," 7, 15,
    60
Declaration of Sentiments and
    Resolutions, 21
DeLauro, Congresswoman
    Rosa L., 73–74, 75
Department of Energy, 85
Department of Housing and
    Urban Development, 86
Dix, Dorothea, 24
Dole, Elizabeth, 14
Dukakis, Michael, 37

E
Elders, Surgeon General
    Joycelyn, 91–93
EMILY's List, 40–42
English, Congresswoman
    Karan, 50–51
Environmental Protection
    Agency (EPA), 14
equality (for women), 15, 17,
    20, 42, 76, 88
Equal Rights Amendment
    (ERA), 76, 109–112

F
Family and Medical Leave Act,
    70–71

Feinstein, Senator Dianne, 55,
    83
Fifteenth Amendment, 27–28
first lady, 94–96
Florida, 42, 49, 60, 62, 89, 90,
    102
Ford, President Gerald, 86
Fourteenth Amendment, 27
Freedom of Choice Act, 66,
    68–70
Fund for the Feminist Majority,
    110
Furse, Congresswoman
    Elizabeth, 62, 63, 64

G
gay(s), 33, 44–45
Georgia, 42, 49, 51
Get Women Elected Now
    (GWEN), 42
Ginsburg, U.S. Supreme Court
    Justice Ruth Bader, 14,
    87–88
Givens, Mayor Linda, 103
governors, women, 10, 104–107
Grimke, Angelina and Sarah,
    19–20

H
Hawaii, 60, 72, 101
Health and Human Services,
    14, 86
Hill, Anita, 12–13, 39
Hilliard, Mayor Patsy Jo, 102
Hornbuckle, Mayor Mary, 102
House Armed Services
    Committee, 45
Hull House, 24
Hutchinson, Senator Kay
    Bailey, 42

I

Idaho, 28, 87
incumbents, 8, 11, 39–40, 105
Indiana, 97, 100, 101
Iowa, 111–112
Ireland, 11

J

Johnson, Congresswoman
    Nancy, 113
Judiciary Committee, 55, 88

K

Kansas, 55, 57, 100
Kassebaum, Senator Nancy, 8,
    55, *56*, 57, 93
Kennedy, Senator Edward, 81,
    83
Kentucky, 97
Ku Klux Klan, 28

L

Landon, Alfred M., 55
League of Women Voters, 31
lesbians, 44–45
Lewis, Ann, 65
Lowell Female Labor Reform
    Association, 25
Lowey, Congresswoman Nita, 41

M

Malcolm, Ellen, 40–41
Martin, Lynn, 14
Maryland, 10, 41, 55, 58
Massachusetts, 22, 24–25, 81
mayors, women, 8–10, 100–104
McKinney, Congresswoman
    Cynthia, 42, *43*, 49, 51
Meek, Congresswoman Carrie,
    49
Mexican Americans, 60

Mikulski, Senator Barbara, 41,
    55, 57–58, *59*, 70
mill workers, 24–25
Mink, Congresswoman Patsy
    T., 60, *61*, 72–73
Minnesota, 86
Missouri, 32, 40, 102, 103
Molinari, Congresswoman
    Susan, 38
Moseley-Braun, Senator Carol,
    49, 51–52, *53*, 54–55
Mott, Lucretia, 20–21
Murray, Senator Patty, 33–34,
    35, 36, 71

N

National Organization for
    Women (NOW), 32, 42,
    69, 110
National Woman Suffrage
    Association, 27
National Women's Political
    Caucus (NWPC), 32, 33,
    71–72
Native Americans, 52, 64
New Jersey, 10, 42, 105
New York, 21, 24, 26, 27, 38,
    41, 60
Nineteenth Amendment, 17,
    26–29, 31
North Carolina, 49, 101
Norton, Congresswoman
    Eleanor Holmes, 8

O

O'Connor, U.S. Supreme
    Court Justice Sandra Day,
    14, 87
Ohio, 22, 60, 76
O'Leary, Secretary of Energy
    Hazel, 14, 85–86

"old boys' club," 47, 51
102nd Congress, 45, 70
103rd Congress, 8, 9, 10, 36, 51, 55
Oregon, 62, 64, 81, 102

P

Pennsylvania, 39, 102
Perkins, Frances, 13–14
Poland, 11
Political Action Committees (PACs), 39, 42
polls, 12, 112
pollster, 105
Power and Money (PAM), 42
Prickett, Mayor Margaret, 101
Pryce, Congresswoman Deborah, 60–62, 76, 77, 78

Q

Quakers, 19–21

R

Reagan, President Ronald, 12, 14, 37, 76, 87, 104
Reno, U.S. Attorney General Janet, 14, 85, 88–91
Republican Network to Elect Women (RENEW), 42
Richards, Governor Ann, 106–107
Roe v. Wade, 66, 68
Roosevelt, Eleanor, 95–96
Roosevelt, President Franklin, 14, 95
Ros-Lehtinen, Congresswoman Ileana, 60
Ross, Nellie Tayloe, 104
Roybal-Allard, Congresswoman Lucille, 60

S

Salter, Susanna Medora, 100
Sayles, Mayor Sharon Belton, 103–104
Schafly, Phyllis, 111
Schroeder, Congresswoman Patricia, 45, 46, 47, 66, 68
Senate Appropriations Committee, 34, 58, 70
Seneca Falls, 21–22
sexual harassment, 13, 45, 47, 58, 66
Shalala, Secretary Donna, 14, 86
slavery, 17, 19–20, 22, 26, 27
Smeal, Eleanor, 110
Smith, Margaret Chase, 32
Snowe, Congresswoman Olympia, 66, 67
Society of Friends, 19. See also Quakers.
South Africa, 52, 54
South Carolina, 19
Specter, Senator Arlen, 39
Stanton, Elizabeth Cady, 20–22, 27
Stone, Lucy, 22, 27

T

Tailhook incident, 45–47
Tennessee, 28
Terry, Mary Sue, 10, 105
Texas, 8, 100, 101, 106
Thomas, U.S. Supreme Court Justice Clarence, 12–13, 39, 55
Truth, Sojourner, 22–23
Turkey, 11
Tyson, Laura D'Andrea, 14

U

United Nations, (UN), 14, 81, 86
United States Capitol, 50
United States Constitution, 17, 27, 29, 109–110
United States House of Representatives, 8, 34, 39, 41, 44, 58, 60
United States Senate, 7–8, 34, 39, 41, 42, 49, 55, 57, 58
United States Supreme Court, 12, 14, 66, 68, 87–88
United States Treasury, 8
Unsoeld, Congresswoman Jolene, 41, 80–81, *82*
Utah, 28

V

Velazquez, Congresswoman Nydia, 60
Virginia, 10, 102, 105
voters, 10, 11, 31, 34, 36, 97–102, 103, 105–106, 111

W

Washington, D.C., 8, 44, 52, 57, 64, 89, 92
Washington (state), 33–34, 36, 41, 62, 80–81, 97, 102
Waters, Congresswoman Maxine, 78, *79*, 80
Weld, Theodore, 20

Whitman, Governor Christine Todd, 10, 105
Willard, Emma, 24
Wilson, Governor Pete, 83
Wilson, President Woodrow, 29
WISH (Women in the Senate and House) List, 42
Woman's Christian Temperance Union, 100
women
  double standard for, 36–37
  governor(s), 10, 104–107
  health equity for, 72–74
  mayor(s), 8–10, 100–104
  in state legislatures, 98–99
  stereotypes, 33, 49–50, 51
  suffrage (right to vote), 8, 17, 19, 22, 27–29, 31, 100
  voters, 31
Women in Power, 37
Women's Health Equity Act of 1991, 72
Woods, Harriet, 32–33, 40
Woolsey, Congresswoman Lynn C., 44–45
World War I, 29
Wyoming, 28, 104

Y

Yeakel, Lynn, 39–40
"Year of the Woman," 7, 104